Belwin's 21st Century

GUITAR CHORD DICTIONARY

by **AARON STANG**

Special thanks to T.J. Bayden of Taylor Guitars for the Taylor Grand Auditorium pictured on the cover.

© 1996 WARNER BROS. PUBLICATIONS
All Rights Reserved

Editor: Aaron Stang
Art Design: Joseph Klucar

Chord Construction

All chords are built from the major scale. **You can figure out the notes in any major scale by applying this pattern of whole- and half-steps: W W H W W W H.** (A half-step is equal to the distance from one fret to the next, a whole step is two frets.)

For example, the A major scale:

> A   B   C#   D   E   F#   G#   A
> W   W   H   W   W   W   H

The scale tones can be numbered:

A	B	C#	D	E	F#	G#	A	B	C#	D	E	F#
1	2	3	4	5	6	7	8	9	10	11	12	13

Any chord can be built from its corresponding major scale by applying the appropriate chord pattern. For example:

Major Chords are built from 1 3 5 of the major scale:

> A major: A C# E

Minor Chords are built from 1 ♭3 5 of the major scale:

> A minor: A C E

Dominant 7th chords are built from 1 3 5 ♭7 of the major scale:

> A7: A C# E G

Note: Since too many notes can sound muddy, and also because we only have four fingers to form chords with, extended chords (chords with 9ths, 11ths and 13ths) often leave out the root (1) or the 5th in order to make room for the rest of the notes. For example:

Dominant 7(♭9) chords are built from 1 3 5 ♭7 ♭9 of the major scale:

> A7(♭9): A C# E G B♭

Often, the actual chord voicing will contain only: C# E G B♭, leaving out the root (A).

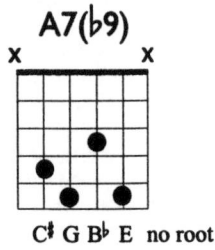

A7(♭9)

C# G B♭ E no root

Here is a complete chord pattern list for all the chord types contained in this book. By applying these patterns to the corresponding major scale (shown at the top of each page) you can figure out the notes in any chord.

Chord Patterns	Examples (Key of A)
Major: 1 3 5	A: A C♯ E
Minor: 1 ♭3 5	Am: A C E
Dominant 7: 1 3 5 ♭7	A7: A C♯ E G
Major 7: 1 3 5 7	Amaj7: A C♯ E G♯
Major 6: 1 3 5 6	A6: A C♯ E F♯
Minor 7: 1 ♭3 5 ♭7	Am7: A C E G
Add 9: 1 3 5 9	A(9): A C♯ E B
Suspended 4: 1 4 5	Asus: A D E
Dominant 9: 1 3 5 ♭7 9	A9: A C♯ E G B
Dominant 13: 1 3 5 ♭7 13	A13: A C♯ E G F♯
Dominant 7(♭9): 1 3 5 ♭7 ♭9	A7(♭9): A C♯ E G B♭
Minor 9: 1 ♭3 5 9	Am9: A C E B
Minor 7(♭5): 1 ♭3 ♭5 ♭7	Am7(♭5): A C E♭ G
Diminished 7: 1 ♭3 ♭5 ♭♭7*(6)	A°7: A C E♭ F♯
Augmented: 1 3 ♯5	A+: A C♯ E♯
Dominant 7(♯5): 1 3 ♯5 ♭7	A7(♯5): A C♯ E♯ G
Dominant 7(♯9): 1 3 5 ♭7 ♯9**(♭3)	A7(♯9): A C♯ E G C

* ♭♭7 = 6
** ♯9 = ♭3

How to Read Chord Frames

A chord frame is a diagram of the guitar neck.

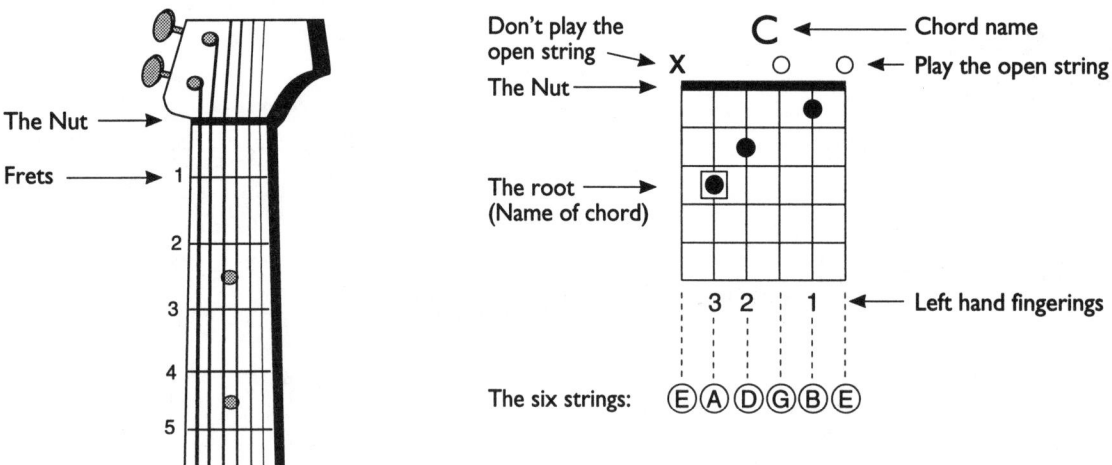

The location of chords played higher up the neck is indicated with a fret number.

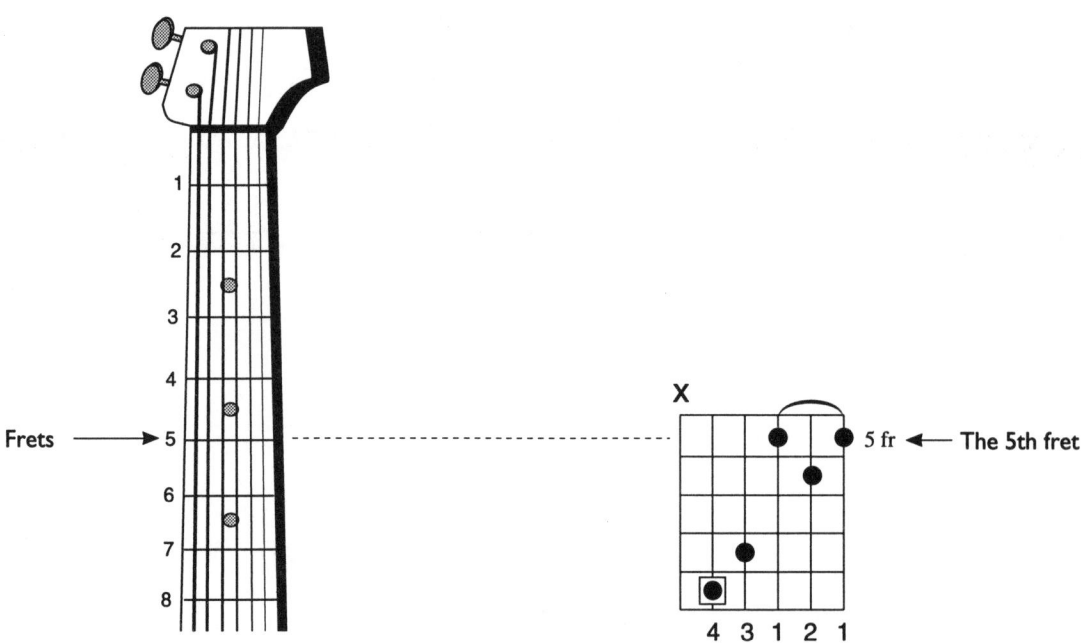

Tears In Heaven

Would you know my name if I saw you in heaven?
Would it be the same if I saw you in heaven?

I must be strong and carry on,
'cause I know I don't belong here in heaven.

Would you hold my hand if I saw you in heaven.
Would ya help me stand if I saw you in heaven?

I'll find my way through night and day,
'cause I know I just can't stay here in heaven.

Time can bring ya down, time can bend your knees.
Time can break your heart, have ya beggin' please, beggin' please.

Beyond the door there's peace, I'm sure,
And I know there'll be no more tears in heaven.

Would you know my name if I saw you in heaven?
Would you be the same if I saw you in heaven?

I'll find my way through night and day,
'cause I know I just can't stay here in heaven.

For Me For You

Time grows heavy upon my mind,
Where are we going, what gets left behind?
And I can feel our precious time,
Slipping away.

For me for you,
It's neither false nor true,
For you for me,
It's only time you see..

Counting the moments
That we share.
Too few and fleeting
It just ain't fair.
Hold me closer,
Until time tears me away.

For me for you,
You know my love is true,
For you for me,
That precious time to be.

Chapters

Taught to hunt the wild ones, at the virgin age of ten,
Calm sense of pride and power, controlling even then,
Barefoot on ocean's aprons, between the long sea grass,
Streaming blonde barechested, arrow readied for the task.

Both heart and waves are pounding, against dark sands of night,
The grasses move, a shot so straight against the still moonlight,
The wild one falls upon the sands, men shout in joyous praise,
The blood of first kill paints, the gentle beauty of her face.

For the leaves are always changing, from green to amber brown,
Life's chapter's are unfolding, pages turning without sound.

Life builds upon that moment, on perfection yet to be,
She leaves her home at sixteen, in her father's old Marquis,
Her music and her innocence, a foundation of raw faith,
Creates the Soul and essence, of a woman full of grace.

The bustle of Chicago, in a row house neighborhood,
Her music leads to marriage, and the joy of motherhood,
Two boys of character are born, and nurtured by her praise,
Calm sense of pride and power, growing steady through their days.

For the leaves are always changing, from green to amber brown,
Life's chapter's are unfolding, pages turning without sound.

In the brilliance of her life's work, a legacy is made,
Respected and admired, by her colleagues and her trade,
Integrity and passion, caring heart in deed and words,
Bring life's joy and happiness, to everyone she serves.

But now a chapter's ending, a blank page yet to write,
She returns to Carolina, and the dark sands of the night,
Barefoot again on aprons, between the long sea grass,
Hand in hand with soulmate, sharing future, sharing past.

For the leaves are always changing, from green to amber brown,
Life's chapter's are unfolding, pages turning without sound,
Yet in her soul's perfection, she knows no time or place,
As the joy of true love paints, the gentle beauty of her face.

Snow Fall

Standing I watch
The falling snow,
And wonder
Why you had to go.

Lonely and cold,
White curtain falls,
Washing away the color,

As I watch you go,
Through falling snow.

Falling Snow.

The firelight warmed,
Your gentle face,
And brought a glow to
A special time and place.

Then something changed,
The firelight died,
Washing away the color,

As I watch you go,
Through falling snow.

Falling Snow.

So now I wait
As true love can,
Wait for the moment
When you fill my heart again.

Such warmth and joy,
As spring returns,
And now the colors they take me,

To your waiting arms,
In falling snow.

No Universe Without You

There is no morning without a sun
no night without a moon.
no sky without a heaven,
no Universe without you.

There is only your depth,
Forever encompassing my world.
There is only your spirit,
Forever teaching me to live again.

There is no heart without your love,
No knowing without your presence,
No feeling without your touch,
No Universe without you.

There is only the morning,
When I see your gentle eyes again.
There is only the night,
Wishing for you to consume me.

There is no feeling without your touch.
There is no Universe without you,
For you have become my very life,
My Universe with you!

Special: A C G
Chorus: Em F C G

How to Use this Book

This book is set up like a dictionary. You can look up chords by locating **the root** (name of the chord) which is shown in a box at the top of each page. Under that box is the corresponding major scale:

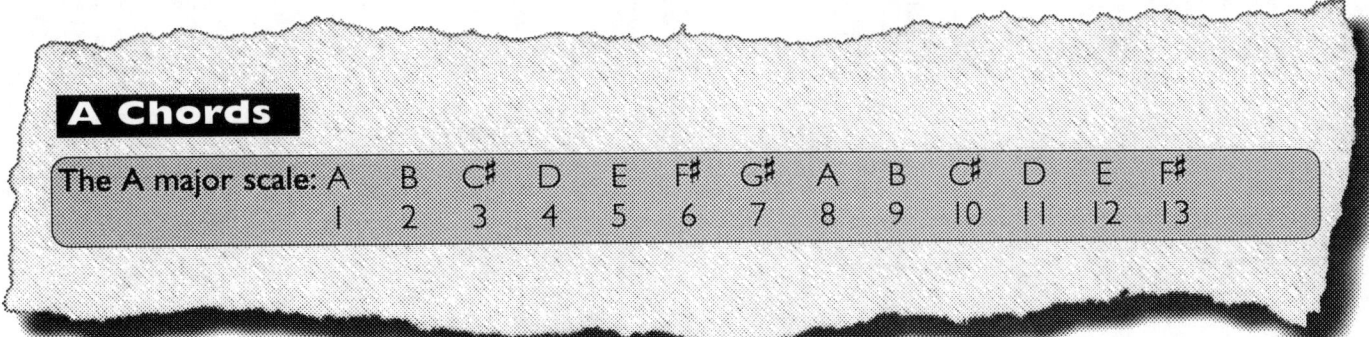

Above each row of chord frames is the chord pattern (formula). You can apply these indicated chord patterns to the major scale to figure out which notes are in that chord:

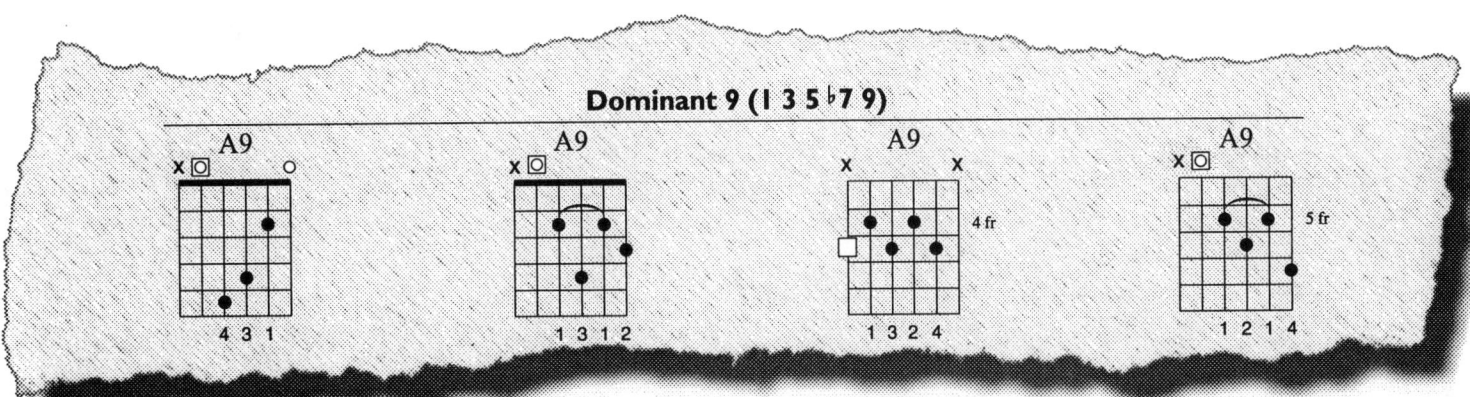

So the notes in an A9 chord are: A C♯ E G B.

The root of every chord is illustrated with a box:

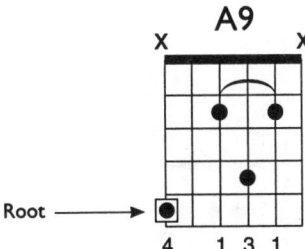

Again, because of voicing limitations some chords don't contain a root. In this case we have indicated the "implied" root with a box (no fingering dot). This is just to assist you in positioning the chord on the neck, don't play this note:

The A major scale:	A	B	C#	D	E	F#	G#	A	B	C#	D	E	F#
	1	2	3	4	5	6	7	8	9	10	11	12	13

Major (1 3 5)

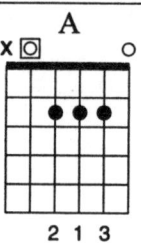 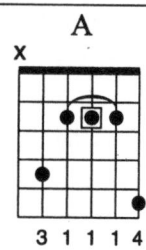 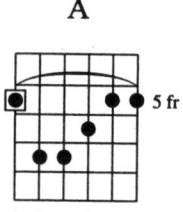 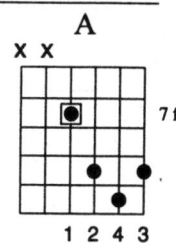

Minor (1 ♭3 5)

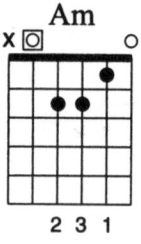 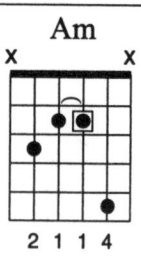 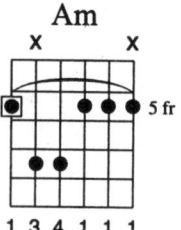 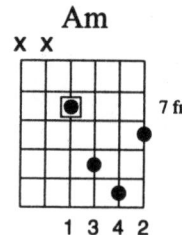

Dominant 7th (1 3 5 ♭7)

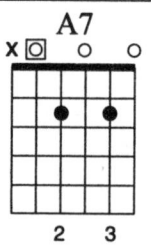 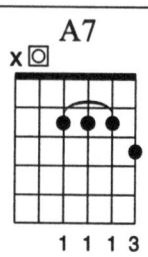 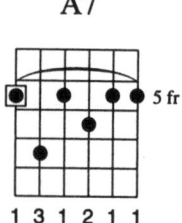 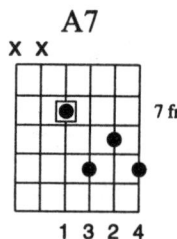

Major 7 (1 3 5 7)

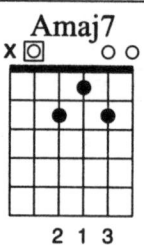 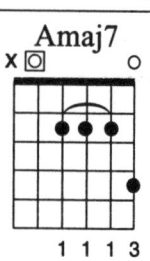 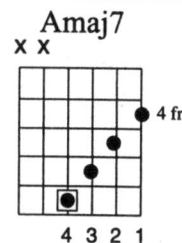 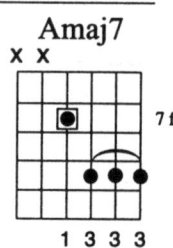

Minor 7th (1 3 5 ♭7)

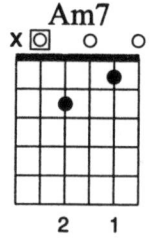 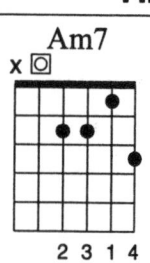 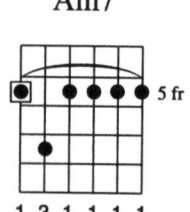 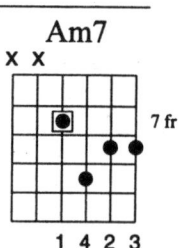

Add 9 (1 3 5 9)

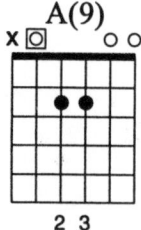 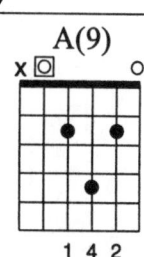

Suspended 4 (1 4 5)

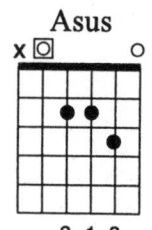 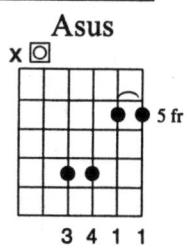

The A major scale:	A	B	C#	D	E	F#	G#	A	B	C#	D	E	F#
	1	2	3	4	5	6	7	8	9	10	11	12	13

Dominant 9 (1 3 5 ♭7 9)

A9
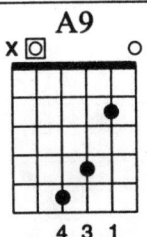

A9
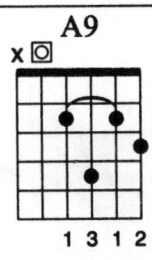

A9
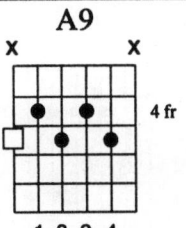

A9
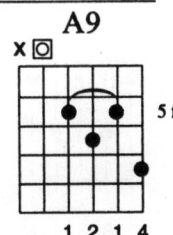

Dominant 13 (1 3 5 ♭7 13)

A13
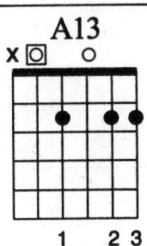

A13
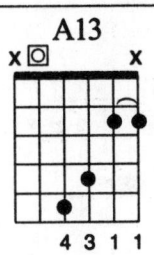

A13
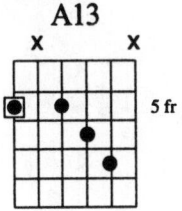

A13
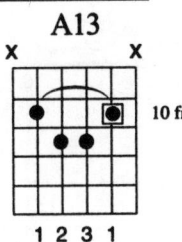

Dominant 7(♭9) (1 3 5 ♭7 ♭9)

A7(♭9)
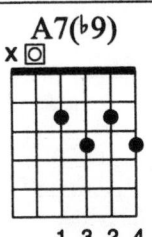

A7(♭9)
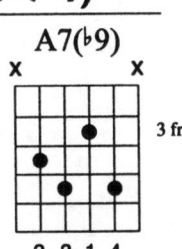

Major 6 (1 3 5 6)

A6
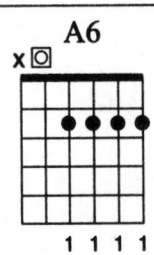

A6
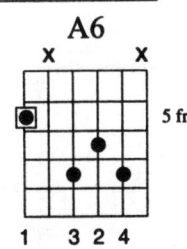

Minor 9 (1 ♭3 5 9)

Am9
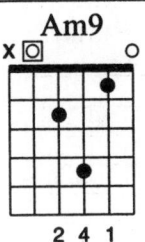

Am9
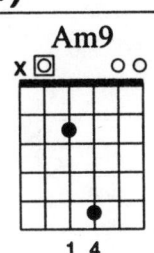

Minor 7(♭5) (1 ♭3 ♭5 ♭7)

Am7(♭5)
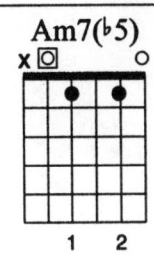

Am7(♭5)
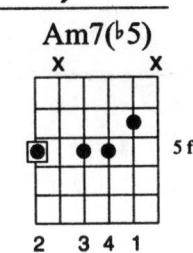

Diminished 7 (1 ♭3 ♭5 ♭♭7)

A°7
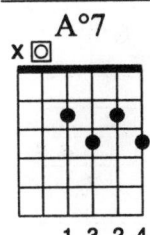

A°7
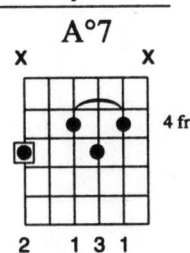

Augmented (1 3 #5)

A+
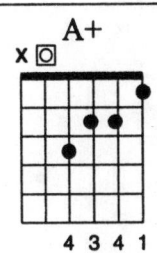

A+
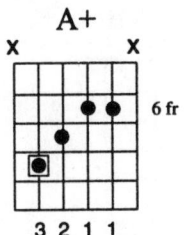

7(#5) (1 3 #5 ♭7)

A7(#5)
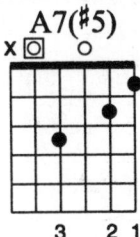

A7(#5)
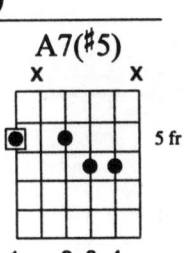

7(#9) (1 3 5 ♭7 #9)

A7(#9)
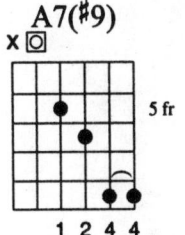

A7(#9)
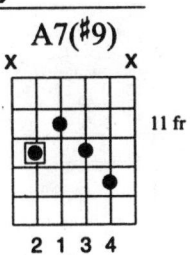

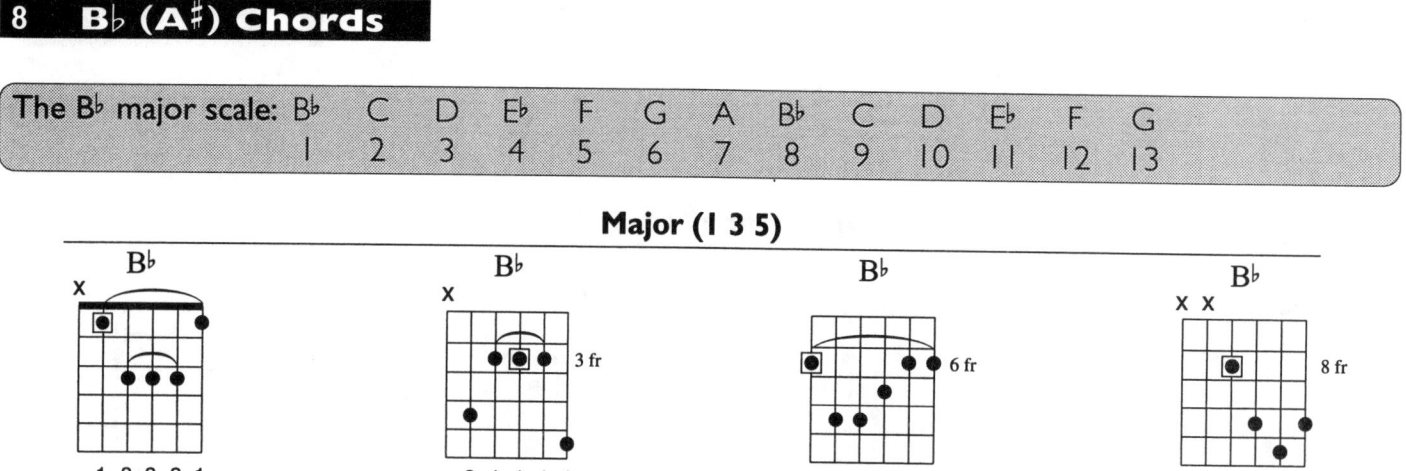

The B♭ major scale:	B♭	C	D	E♭	F	G	A	B♭	C	D	E♭	F	G
	1	2	3	4	5	6	7	8	9	10	11	12	13

Major (1 3 5)

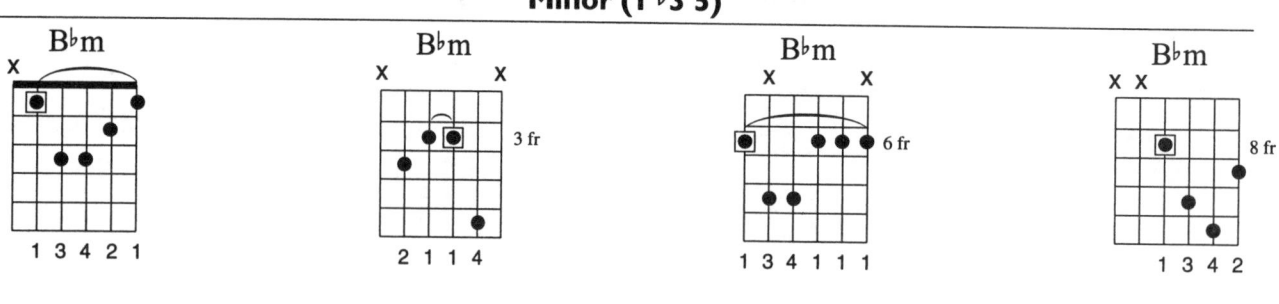

Minor (1 ♭3 5)

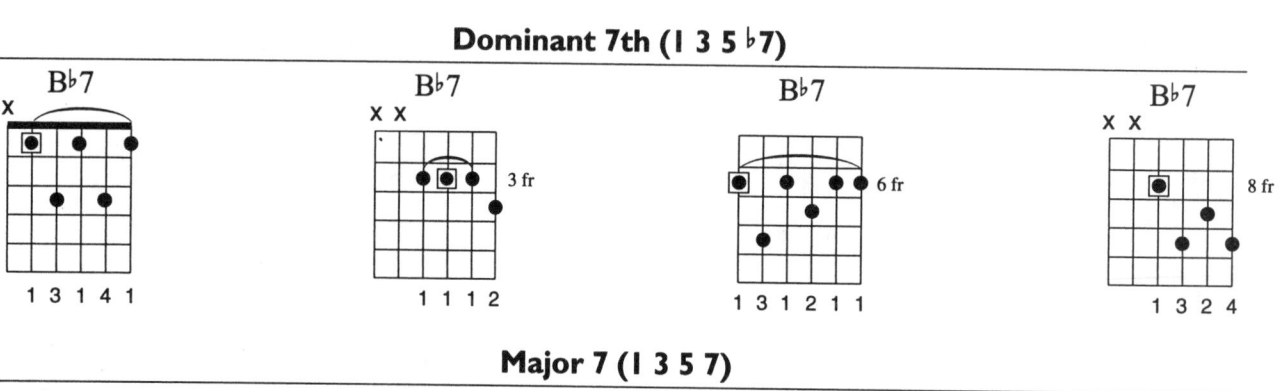

Dominant 7th (1 3 5 ♭7)

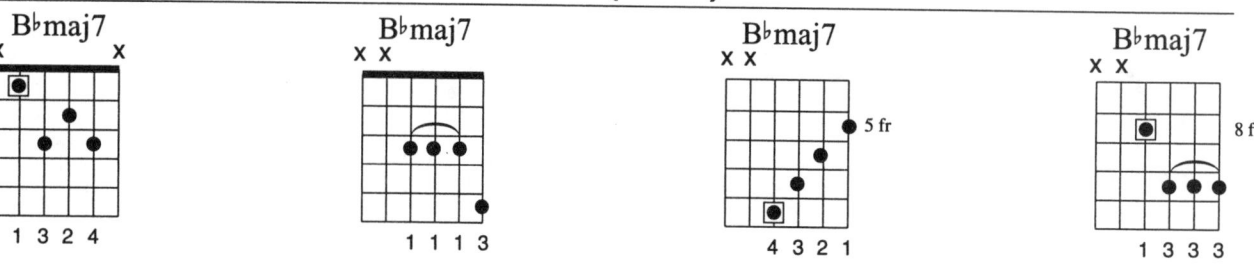

Major 7 (1 3 5 7)

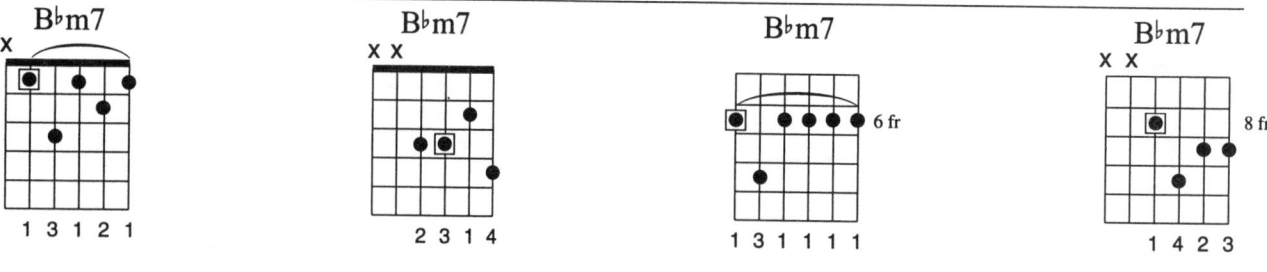

Minor 7th (1 3 5 ♭7)

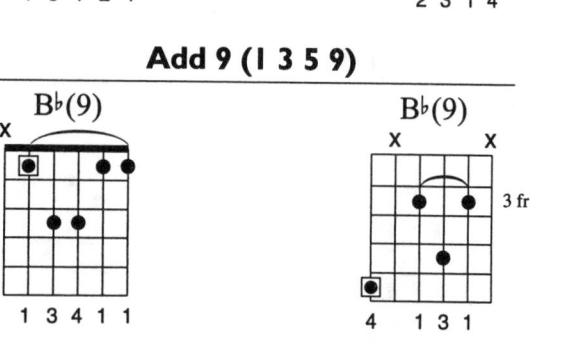

Add 9 (1 3 5 9)

Suspended 4

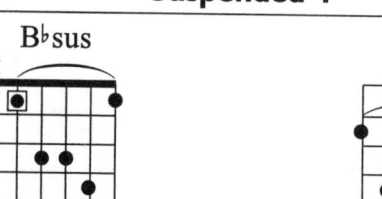

The B♭ major scale:	B♭	C	D	E♭	F	G	A	B♭	C	D	E♭	F	G
	1	2	3	4	5	6	7	8	9	10	11	12	13

Dominant 9 (1 3 5 ♭7 9)

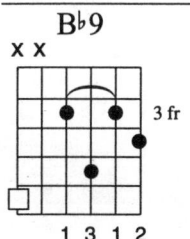
B♭9

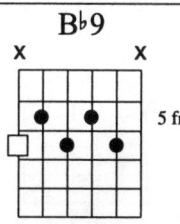
B♭9

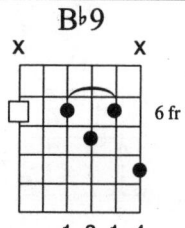
B♭9

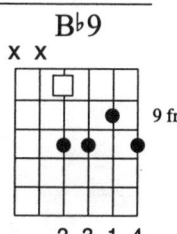
B♭9

Dominant 13 (1 3 5 ♭7 13)

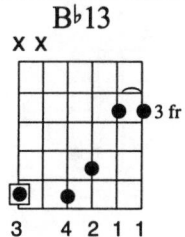
B♭13

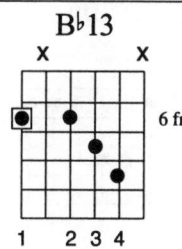
B♭13

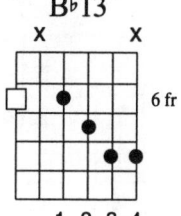
B♭13

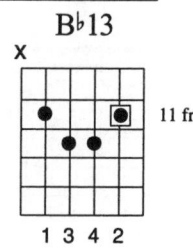
B♭13

Dominant 7(♭9) (1 3 5 ♭7 ♭9)

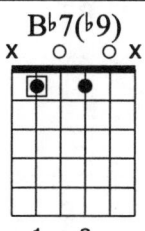
B♭7(♭9)

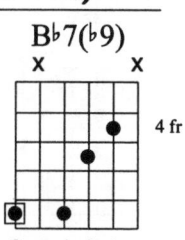
B♭7(♭9)

Major 6 (1 3 5 6)

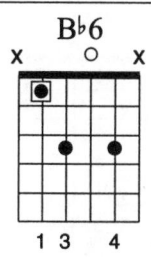
B♭6

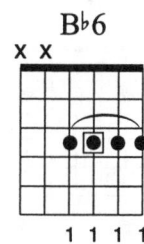
B♭6

Minor 9 (1 ♭3 5 9)

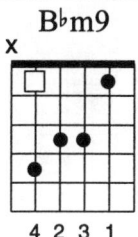
B♭m9

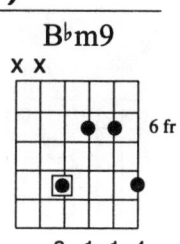
B♭m9

Minor 7(♭5) (1 ♭3 ♭5 ♭7)

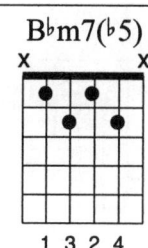
B♭m7(♭5)

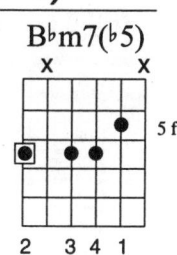
B♭m7(♭5)

Diminished 7 (1 ♭3 ♭5 ♭♭7)

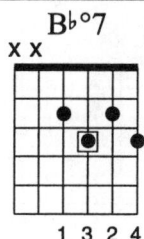
B♭°7

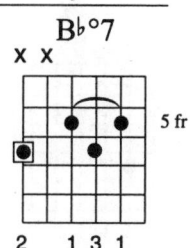
B♭°7

Augmented (1 3 ♯5)

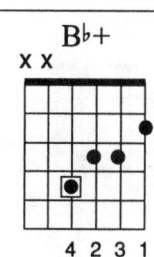
B♭+

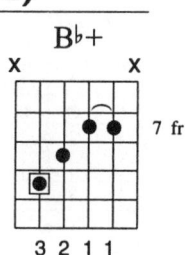
B♭+

7(♯5) (1 3 ♯5 ♭7)

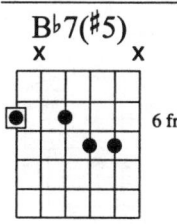
B♭7(♯5)

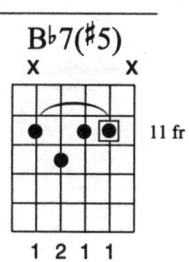
B♭7(♯5)

7(♯9) (1 3 5 ♭7 ♯9)

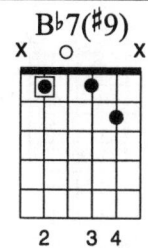
B♭7(♯9)

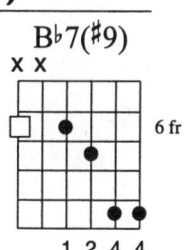
B♭7(♯9)

The B major scale:	B	C#	D	E	F#	G#	A	B	C#	D	E	F#	G#
	1	2	3	4	5	6	7	8	9	10	11	12	13

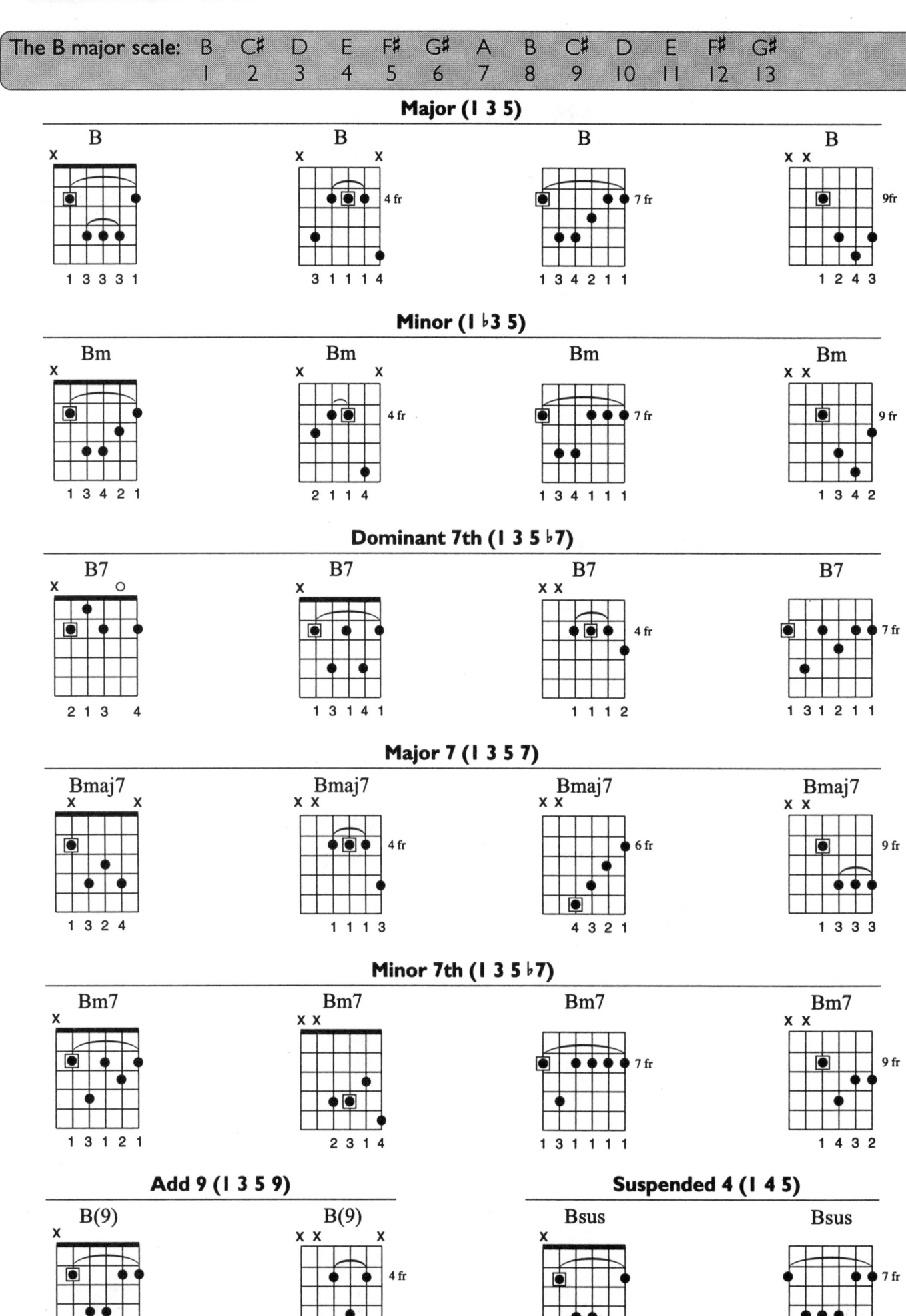

Major (1 3 5)

Minor (1 ♭3 5)

Dominant 7th (1 3 5 ♭7)

Major 7 (1 3 5 7)

Minor 7th (1 3 5 ♭7)

Add 9 (1 3 5 9)   ### Suspended 4 (1 4 5)

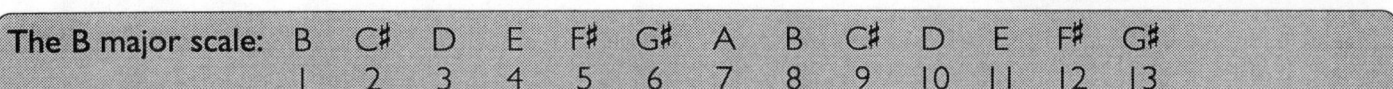

The B major scale:	B	C#	D	E	F#	G#	A	B	C#	D	E	F#	G#
	1	2	3	4	5	6	7	8	9	10	11	12	13

Dominant 9 (1 3 5 ♭7 9)

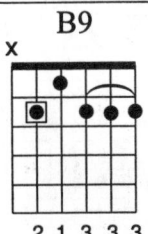
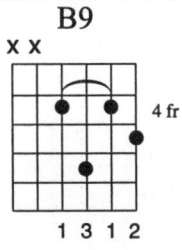
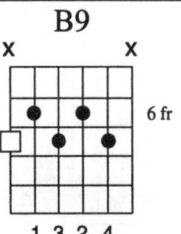
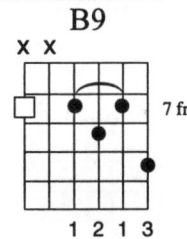

Dominant 13 (1 3 5 ♭7 13)

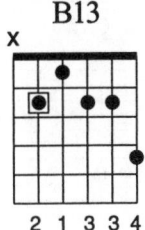
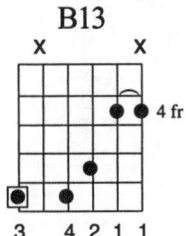
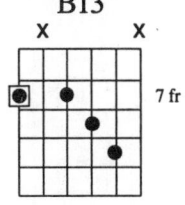
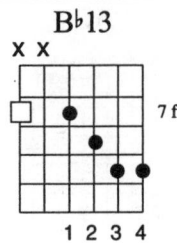

Dominant 7(♭9) (1 3 5 ♭7 ♭9)   ## Major 6 (1 3 5 6)

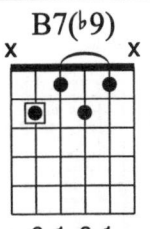
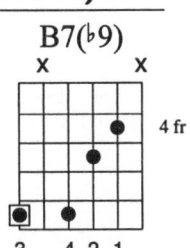
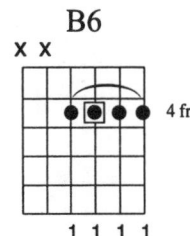
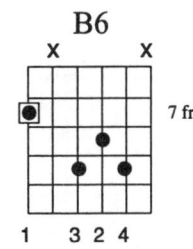

Minor 9 (1 ♭3 5 9)   ## Minor 7(♭5) (1 ♭3 ♭5 ♭7)

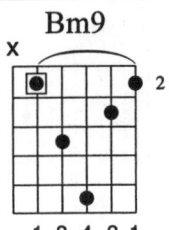
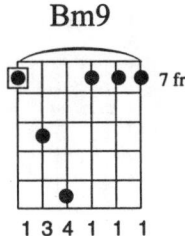
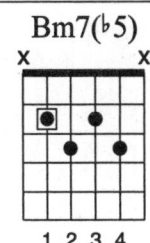
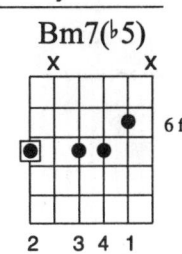

Diminished 7 (1 ♭3 ♭5 ♭♭7)   ## Augmented (1 3 #5)

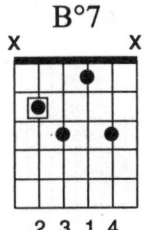
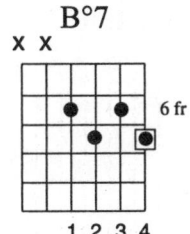
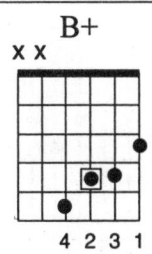
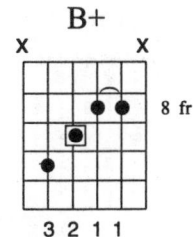

7(#5) (1 3 #5 ♭7)   ## 7(#9) (1 3 5 ♭7 #9)

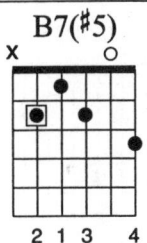
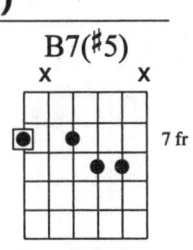
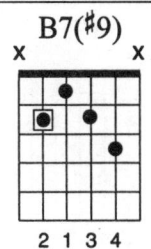
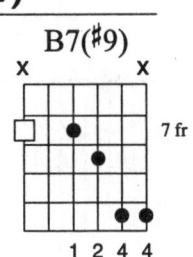

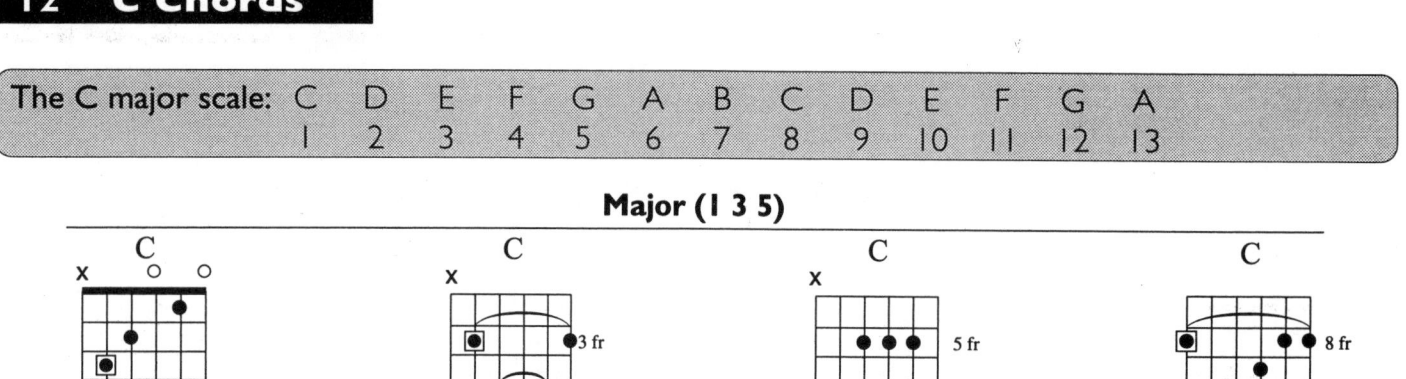

The C major scale:

C	D	E	F	G	A	B	C	D	E	F	G	A
1	2	3	4	5	6	7	8	9	10	11	12	13

Major (1 3 5)

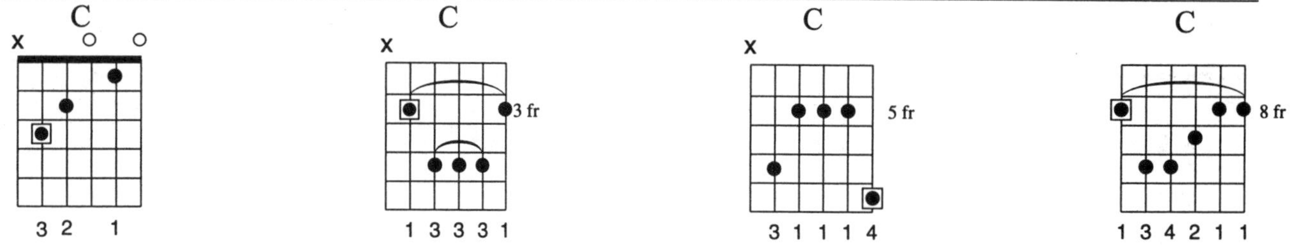

Minor (1 ♭3 5)

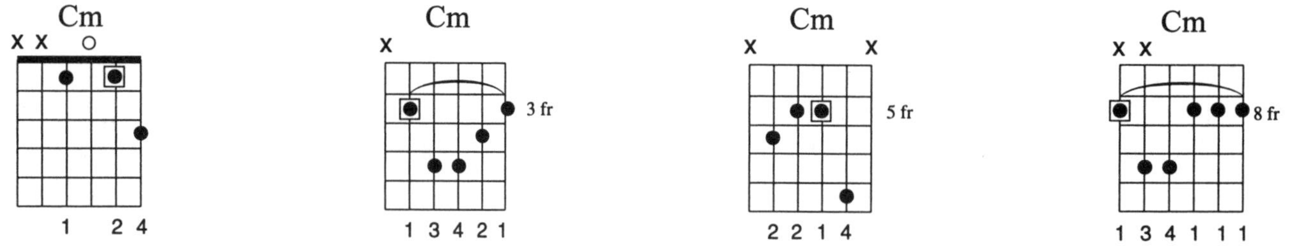

Dominant 7th (1 3 5 ♭7)

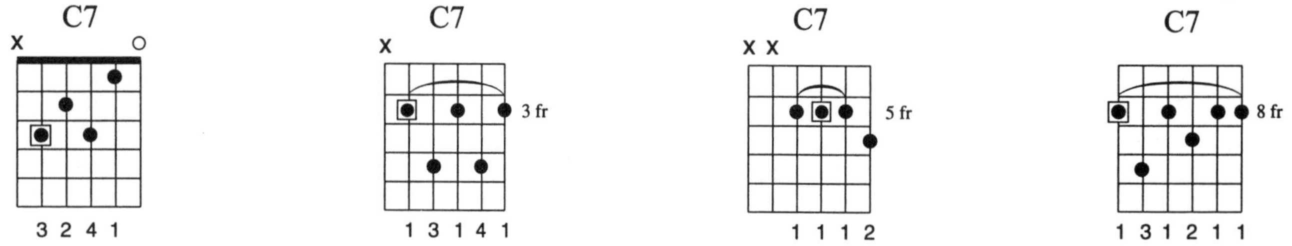

Major 7 (1 3 5 7)

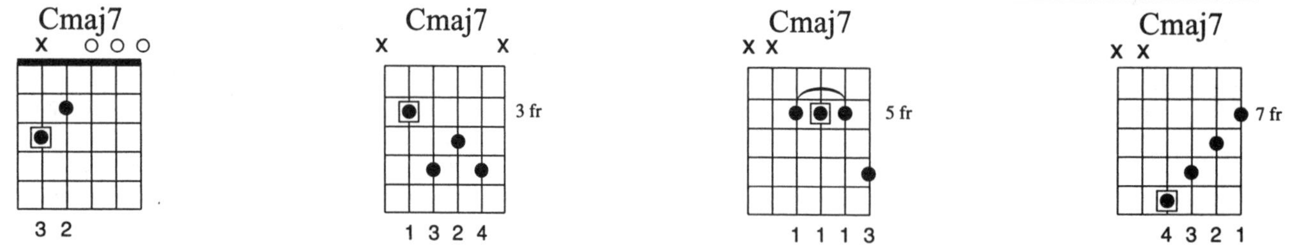

Minor 7th (1 ♭3 5 ♭7)

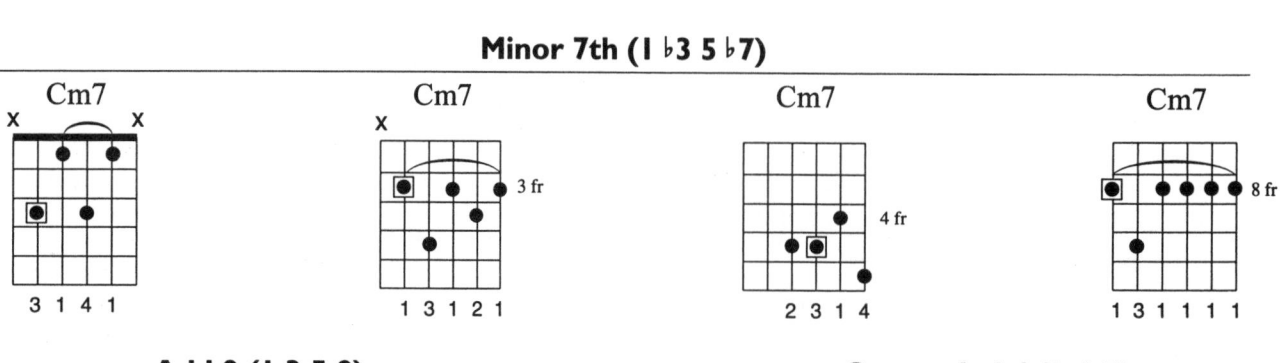

Add 9 (1 3 5 9)

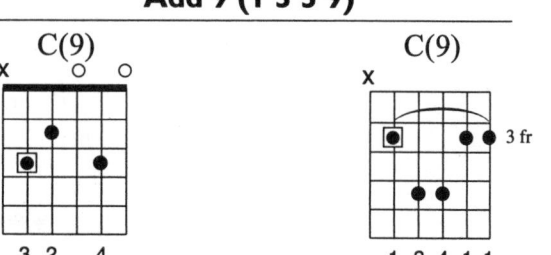

Suspended 4 (1 4 5)

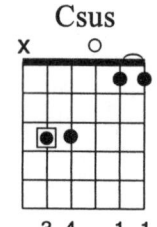
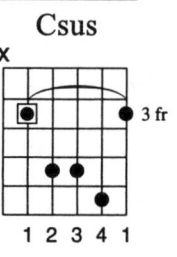

The C major scale:	C	D	E	F	G	A	B	C	D	E	F	G	A
	1	2	3	4	5	6	7	8	9	10	11	12	13

Dominant 9 (1 3 5 ♭7 9)

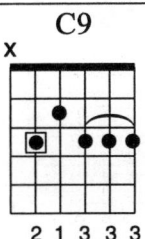
C9

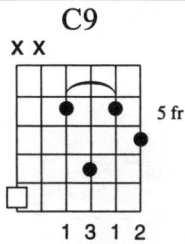
C9
5 fr

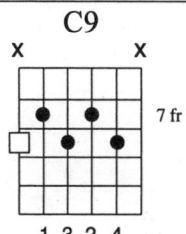
C9
7 fr

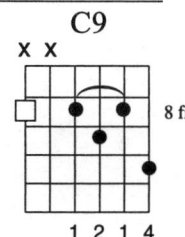
C9
8 fr

Dominant 13 (1 3 5 ♭7 13)

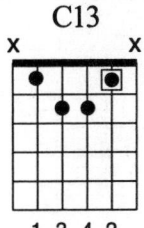
C13

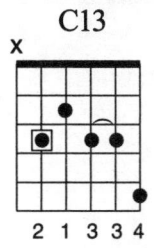
C13

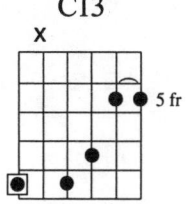
C13
5 fr

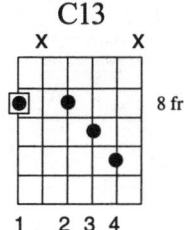
C13
8 fr

Dominant 7(♭9) (1 3 5 ♭7 ♭9)

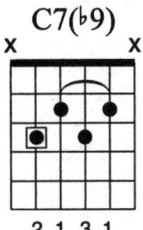
C7(♭9)

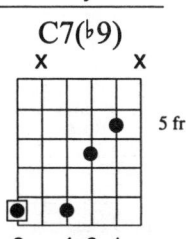
C7(♭9)
5 fr

Major 6 (1 3 5 6)

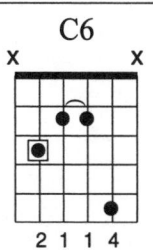
C6

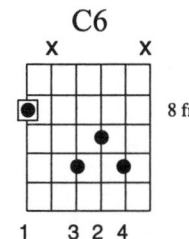
C6
8 fr

Minor 9 (1 ♭3 5 9)

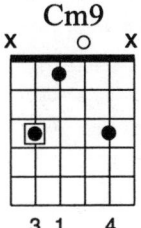
Cm9

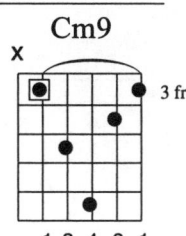
Cm9
3 fr

Minor 7(♭5) (1 ♭3 ♭5 ♭7)

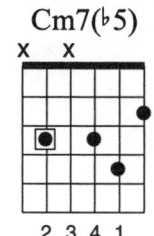
Cm7(♭5)

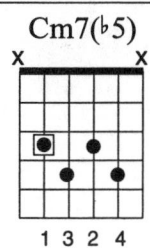
Cm7(♭5)

Diminished 7 (1 ♭3 ♭5 ♭♭7)

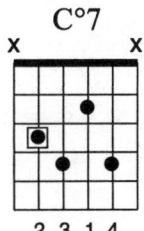
C°7

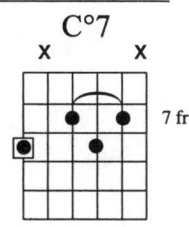
C°7
7 fr

Augmented (1 3 ♯5)

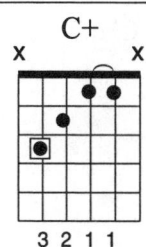
C+

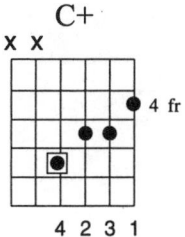
C+
4 fr

7(♯5) (1 3 ♯5 ♭7)

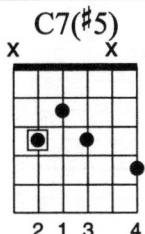
C7(♯5)

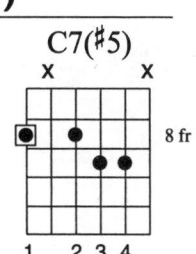
C7(♯5)
8 fr

7(♯9) (1 3 5 ♭7 ♯9)

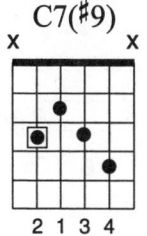
C7(♯9)

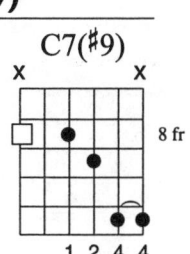
C7(♯9)
8 fr

The C♯ major scale:

C♯	D♯	E♯	F♯	G♯	A♯	B♯	C♯	D♯	E♯	F♯	G♯	A♯
1	2	3	4	5	6	7	8	9	10	11	12	13

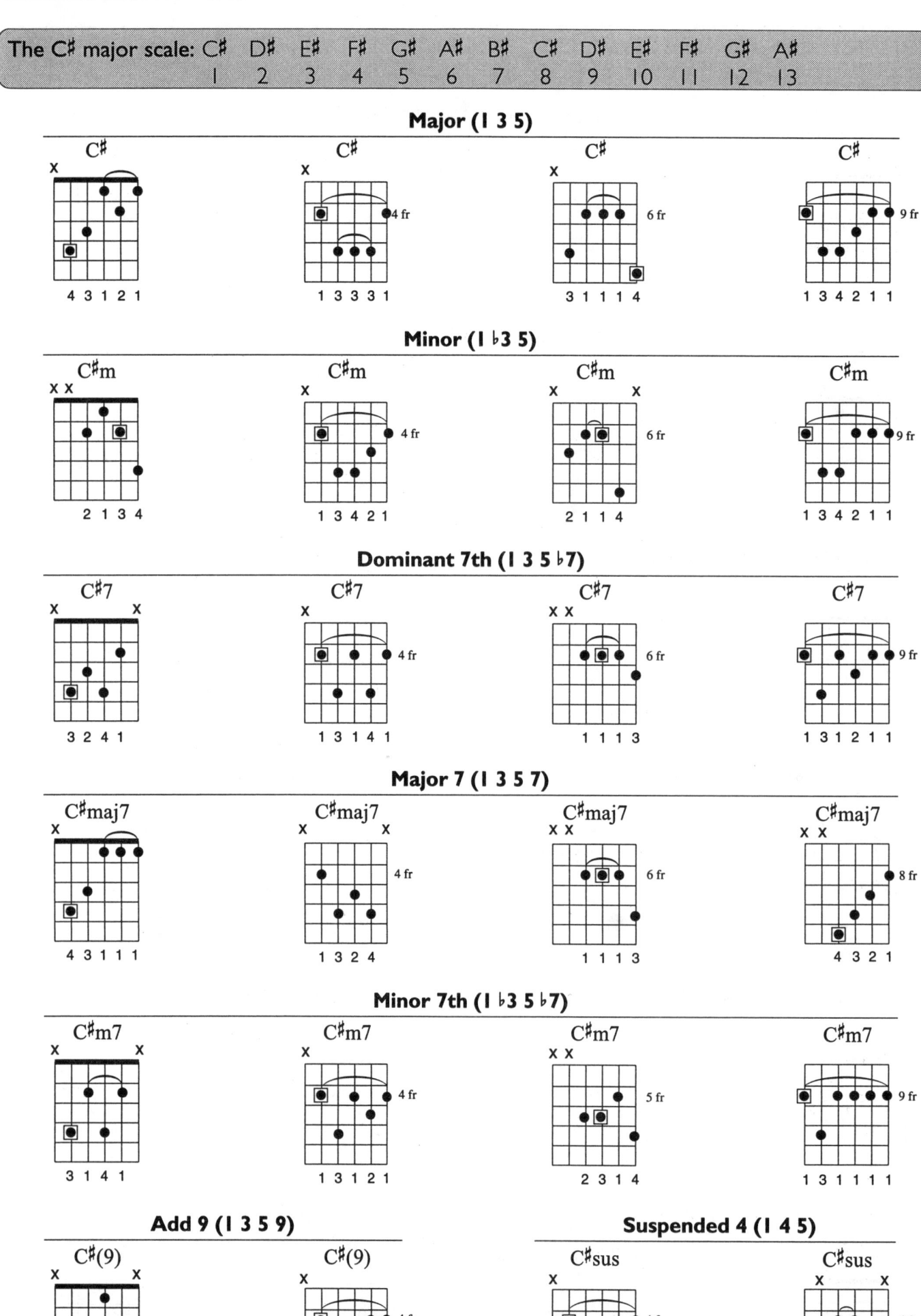

The C♯ major scale:	C♯	D♯	E♯	F♯	G♯	A♯	B♯	C♯	D♯	E♯	F♯	G♯	A♯
	1	2	3	4	5	6	7	8	9	10	11	12	13

Dominant 9 (1 3 5 ♭7 9)

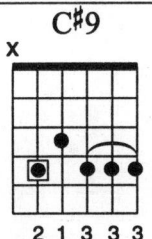
C♯9

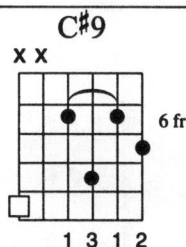
C♯9

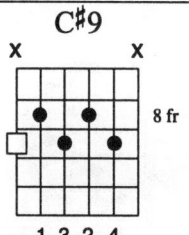
C♯9

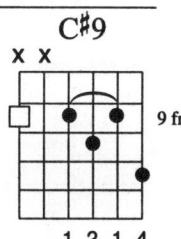
C♯9

Dominant 13 (1 3 5 ♭7 13)

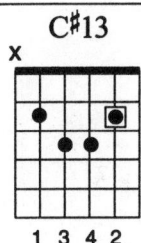
C♯13

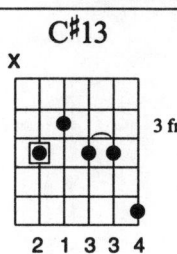
C♯13

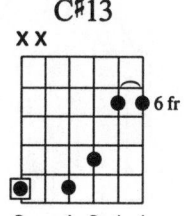
C♯13

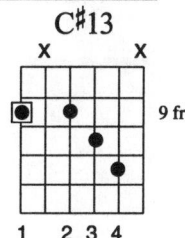
C♯13

Dominant 7(♭9) (1 3 5 ♭7 ♭9)

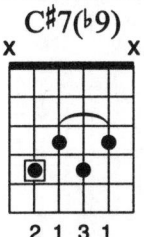
C♯7(♭9)

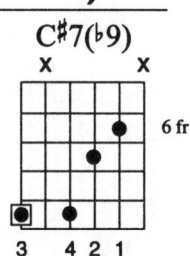
C♯7(♭9)

Major 6 (1 3 5 6)

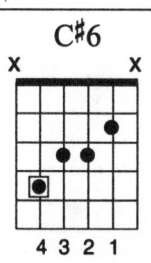
C♯6

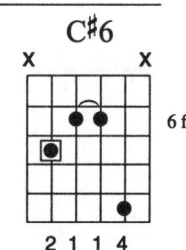
C♯6

Minor 9 (1 ♭3 5 9)

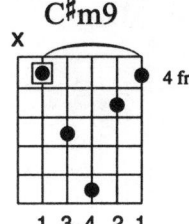
C♯m9

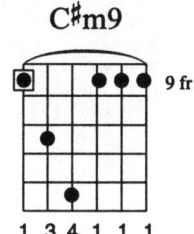
C♯m9

Minor 7(♭5) (1 ♭3 ♭5 ♭7)

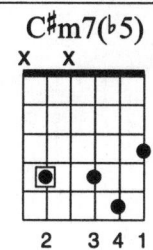
C♯m7(♭5)

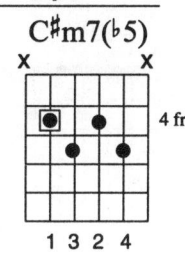
C♯m7(♭5)

Diminished 7 (1 ♭3 ♭5 ♭♭7)

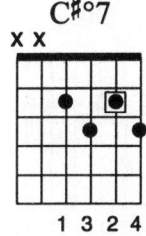
C♯°7

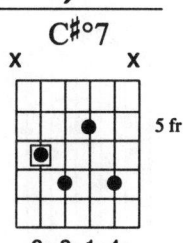
C♯°7

Augmented (1 3 ♯5)

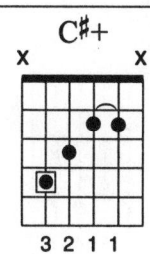
C♯+

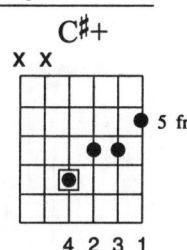
C♯+

7(♯5) (1 3 ♯5 ♭7)

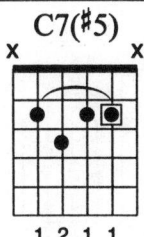
C7(♯5)

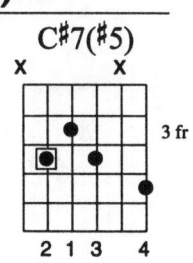
C♯7(♯5)

7(♯9) (1 3 5 ♭7 ♯9)

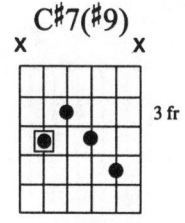
C♯7(♯9)

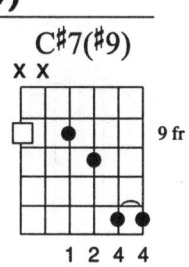
C♯7(♯9)

The D major scale:	D	E	F#	G	A	B	C#	D	E	F#	G	A	B
	1	2	3	4	5	6	7	8	9	10	11	12	13

Major (1 3 5)

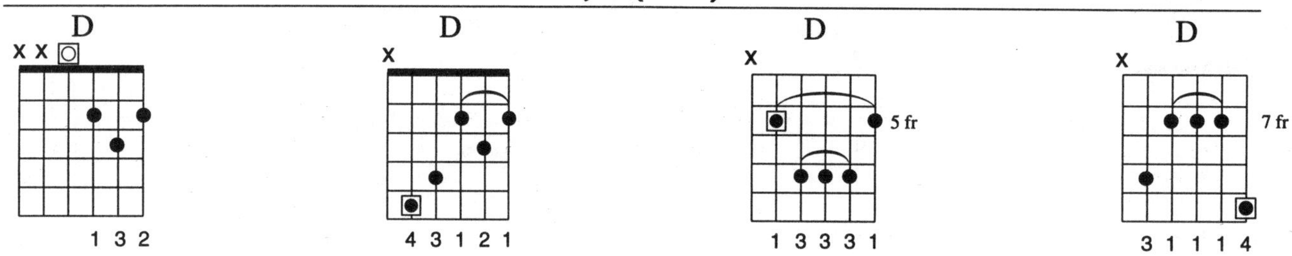

D   **D**   **D**   **D**

Minor (1 ♭3 5)

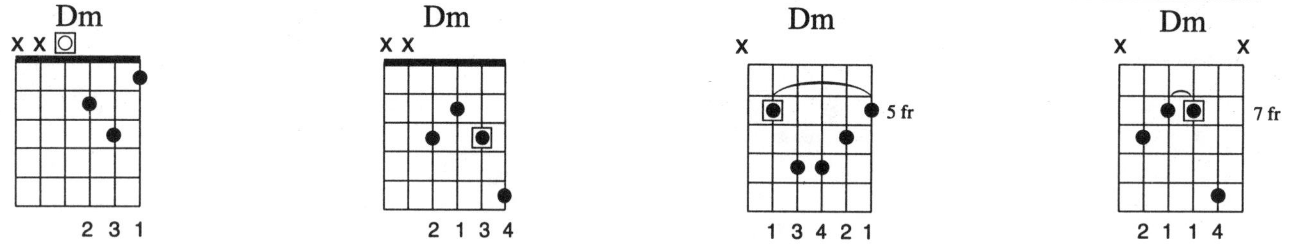

Dm   **Dm**   **Dm**   **Dm**

Dominant 7th (1 3 5 ♭7)

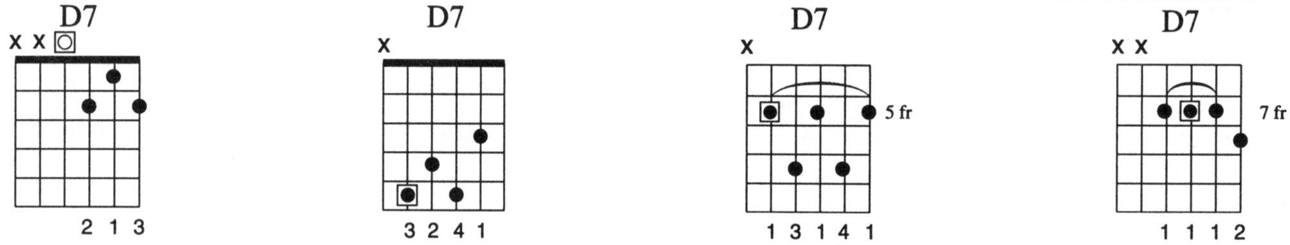

D7   **D7**   **D7**   **D7**

Major 7 (1 3 5 7)

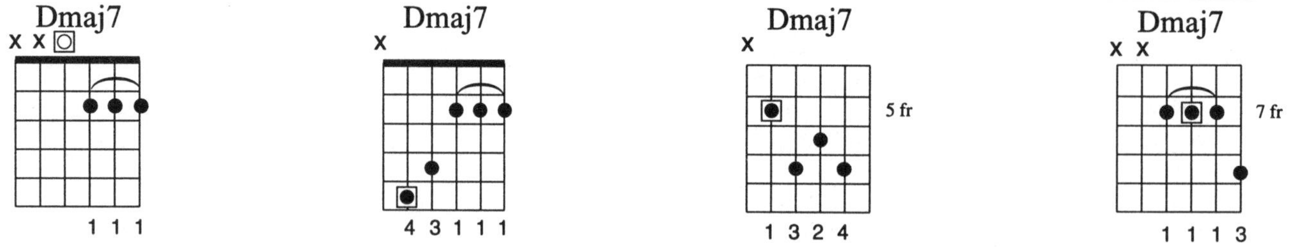

Dmaj7   **Dmaj7**   **Dmaj7**   **Dmaj7**

Minor 7th (1 ♭3 5 ♭7)

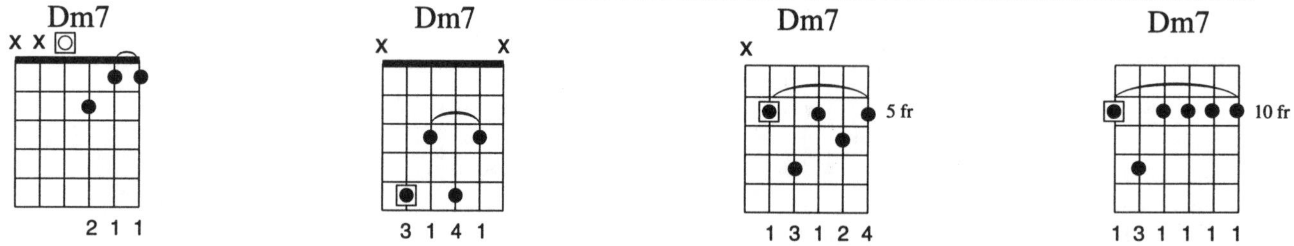

Dm7   **Dm7**   **Dm7**   **Dm7**

Add 9 (1 3 5 9)

D(9)   **D(9)**

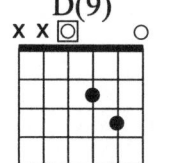
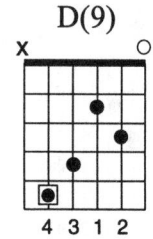

Suspended 4 (1 4 5)

Dsus   **Dsus**

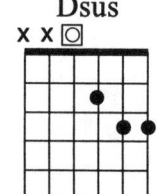
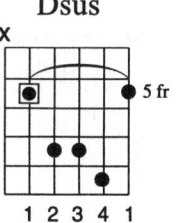

The D major scale:	D	E	F#	G	A	B	C#	D	E	F#	G	A	B
	1	2	3	4	5	6	7	8	9	10	11	12	13

Dominant 9 (1 3 5 ♭7 9)

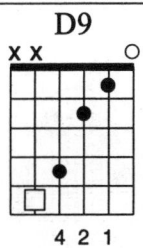
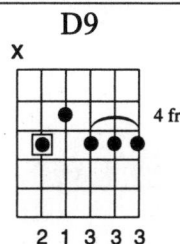
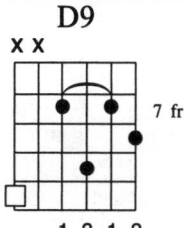
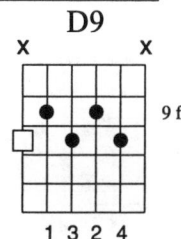

Dominant 13 (1 3 5 ♭7 13)

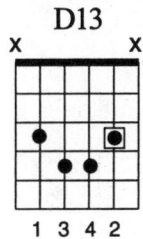
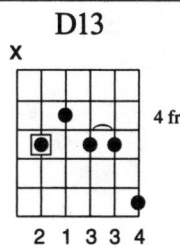
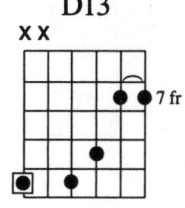
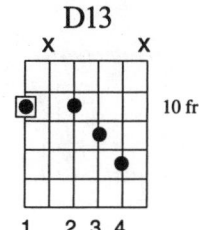

Dominant 7(♭9) (1 3 5 ♭7 ♭9)

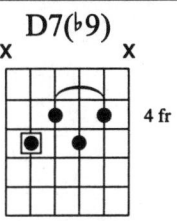
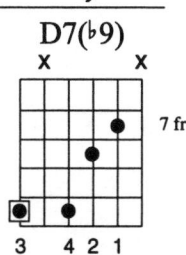

Major 6 (1 3 5 6)

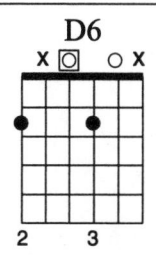
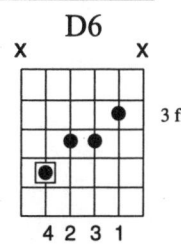

Minor 9 (1 ♭3 5 9)

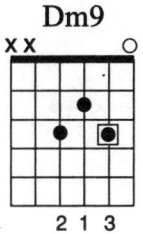
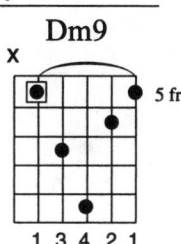

Minor 7(♭5) (1 ♭3 ♭5 ♭7)

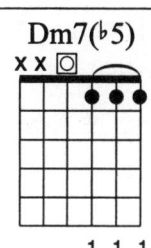
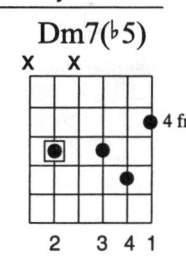

Diminished 7 (1 ♭3 ♭5 ♭♭7)

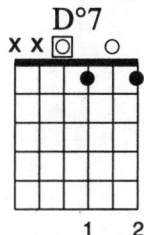
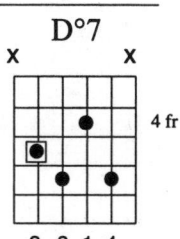

Augmented (1 3 #5)

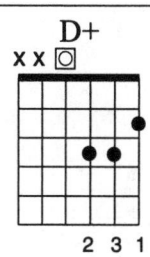
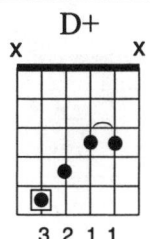

7(#5) (1 3 #5 ♭7)

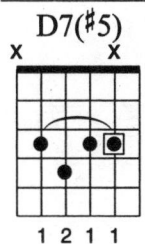
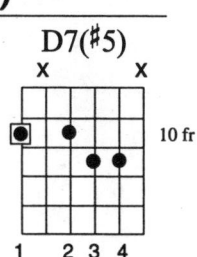

7(#9) (1 3 5 ♭7 #9)

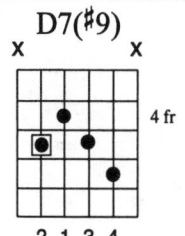
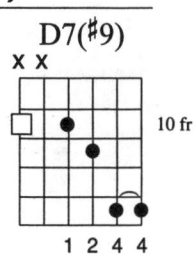

The E♭ major scale:	E♭	F	G	A♭	B♭	C	D	E♭	F	G	A♭	B♭	C
	1	2	3	4	5	6	7	8	9	10	11	12	13

Major (1 3 5)

E♭

x x

1 2 4 3

E♭

x

3 fr

4 3 1 2 1

E♭

x

6 fr

1 3 3 3 1

E♭

x

8 fr

3 1 1 1 4

Minor (1 ♭3 5)

E♭m

x x

1 3 4 2

E♭m

x x

3 fr

2 1 3 4

E♭m

x

6 fr

1 3 4 2 1

E♭m

x   x

8 fr

2 1 1 4

Dominant 7th (1 3 5 ♭7)

E♭7

x x

1 3 2 4

E♭7

x   x

4 fr

3 2 4 1

E♭7

x

6 fr

1 3 1 4 1

E♭7

x x

8 fr

1 1 1 2

Major 7 (1 3 5 7)

E♭maj7

x x

1 3 3 3

E♭maj7

x

3 fr

4 3 1 1 1

E♭maj7

x   x

6 fr

1 3 2 4

E♭maj7

x x

8 fr

1 1 1 3

Minor 7th (1 ♭3 5 ♭7)

E♭m7

x x

1 4 2 3

E♭m7

x   x

4 fr

3 1 4 1

E♭m7

x

6 fr

1 3 1 2 1

E♭m7

x x

7 fr

2 3 1 4

Add 9 (1 3 5 9)

E♭(9)

x x

1 3 4 1

E♭(9)

x   x

3 fr

3 2 1 4

Suspended 4 (1 4 5)

E♭sus

x

6 fr

1 2 3 4 1

E♭sus

x   x

6 fr

4   1 1 2

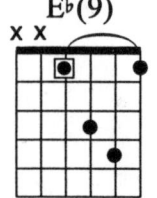
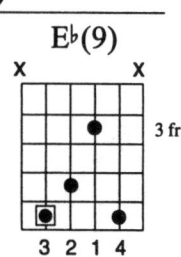
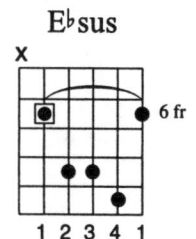
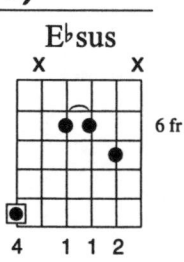

The E♭ major scale:	E♭	F	G	A♭	B♭	C	D	E♭	F	G	A♭	B♭	C
	1	2	3	4	5	6	7	8	9	10	11	12	13

Dominant 9 (1 3 5 ♭7 9)

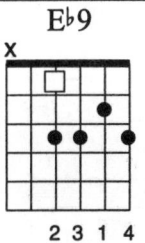
E♭9

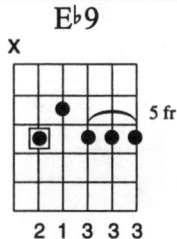
E♭9

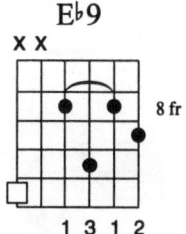
E♭9

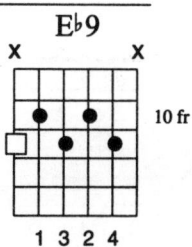
E♭9

Dominant 13 (1 3 5 ♭7 13)

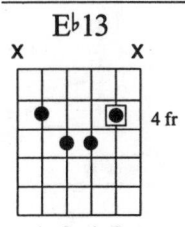
E♭13

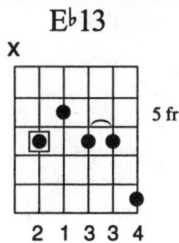
E♭13

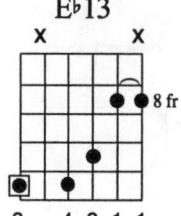
E♭13

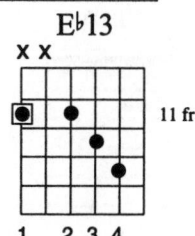
E♭13

Dominant 7(♭9) (1 3 5 ♭7 ♭9)   ## Major 6 (1 3 5 6)

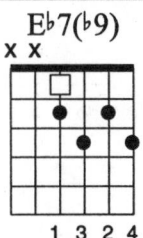
E♭7(♭9)

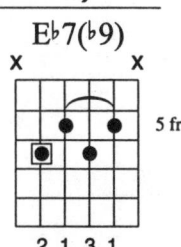
E♭7(♭9)

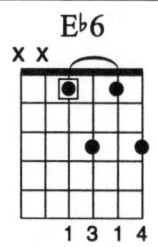
E♭6

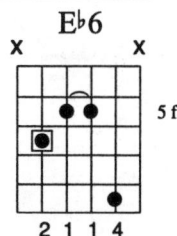
E♭6

Minor 9 (1 ♭3 5 9)   ## Minor 7(♭5) (1 ♭3 ♭5 ♭7)

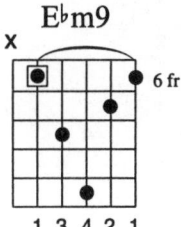
E♭m9

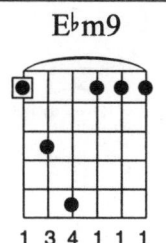
E♭m9

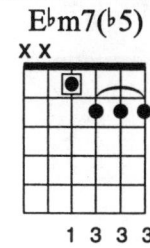
E♭m7(♭5)

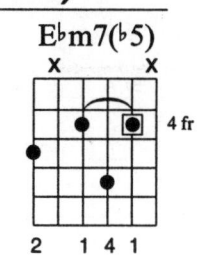
E♭m7(♭5)

Diminished 7 (1 ♭3 ♭5 ♭♭7)   ## Augmented (1 3 ♯5)

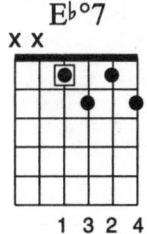
E♭°7

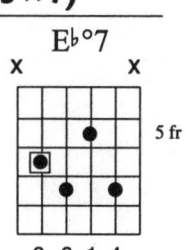
E♭°7

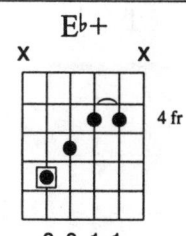
E♭+

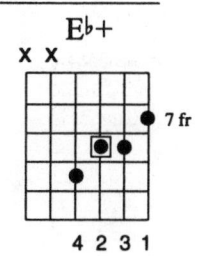
E♭+

7(♯5) (1 3 ♯5 ♭7)   ## 7(♯9) (1 3 5 ♭7 ♯9)

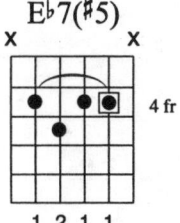
E♭7(♯5)

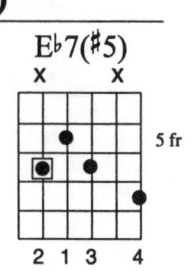
E♭7(♯5)

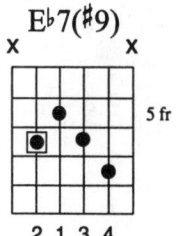
E♭7(♯9)

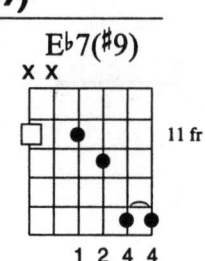
E♭7(♯9)

The E major scale:	E	F#	G#	A	B	C#	D#	E	F#	G#	A	B	C#
	1	2	3	4	5	6	7	8	9	10	11	12	13

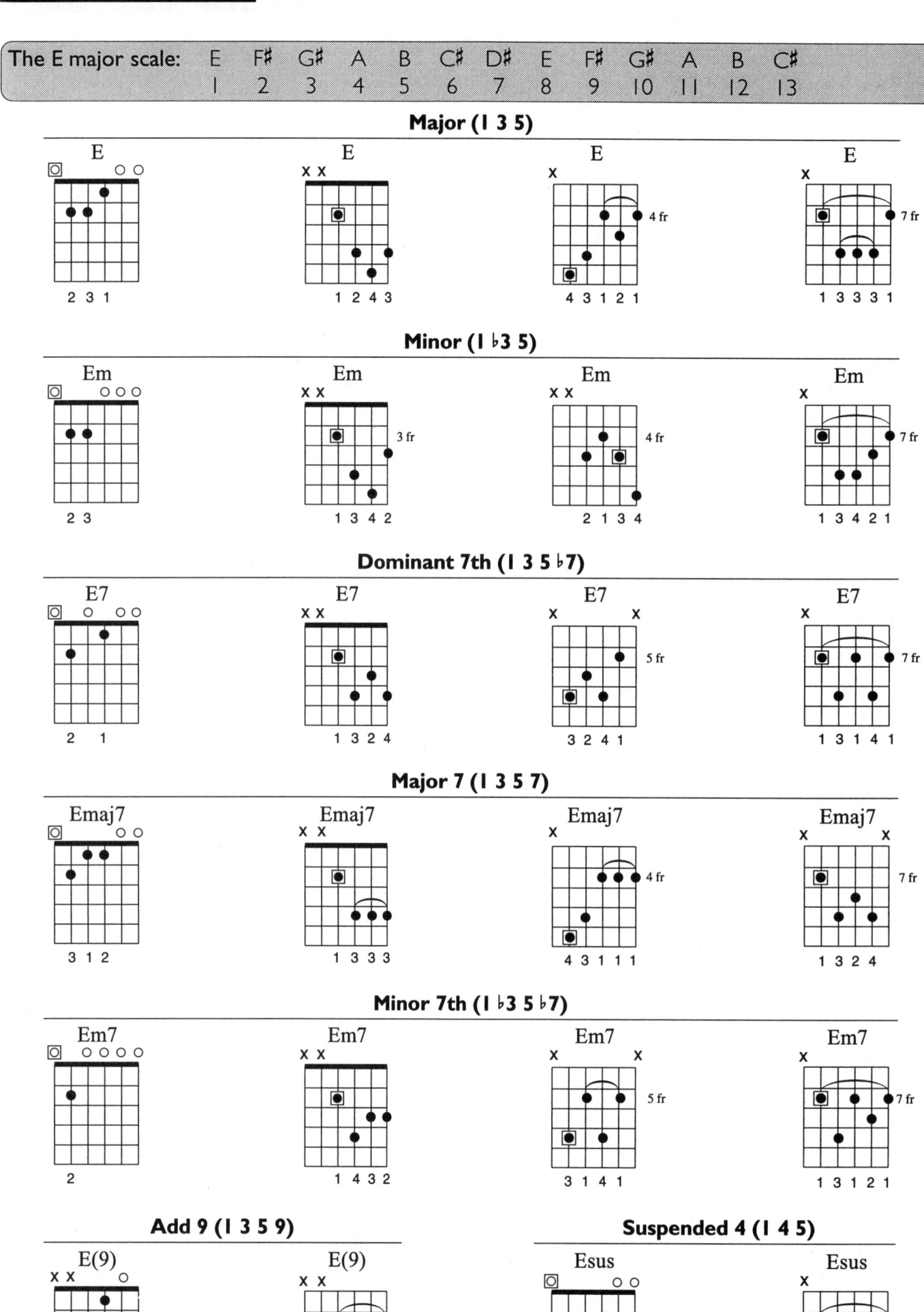

The E major scale:	E	F#	G#	A	B	C#	D#	E	F#	G#	A	B	C#
	1	2	3	4	5	6	7	8	9	10	11	12	13

Dominant 9 (1 3 5 ♭7 9)

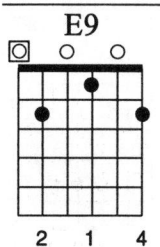
E9

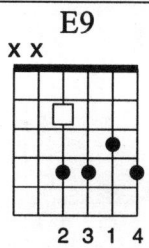
E9

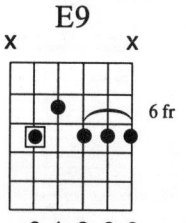
E9
6 fr

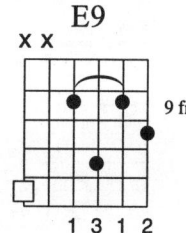
E9
9 fr

Dominant 13 (1 3 5 ♭7 13)

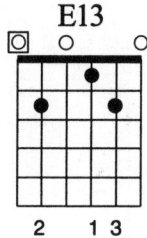
E13

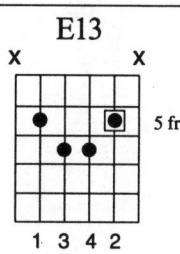
E13
5 fr

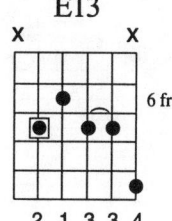
E13
6 fr

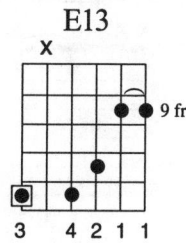
E13
9 fr

Dominant 7(♭9) (1 3 5 ♭7 ♭9)

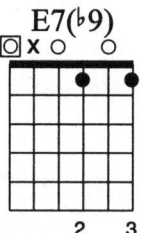
E7(♭9)

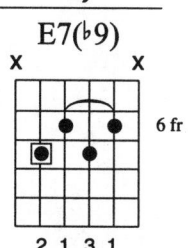
E7(♭9)
6 fr

Major 6 (1 3 5 6)

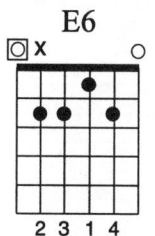
E6

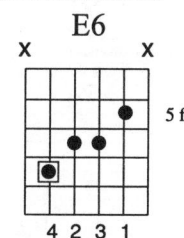
E6
5 fr

Minor 9 (1 ♭3 5 9)

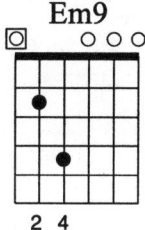
Em9

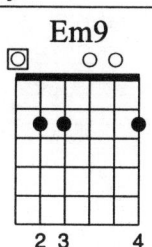
Em9

Minor 7(♭5) (1 ♭3 ♭5 ♭7)

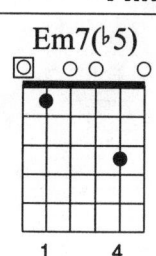
Em7(♭5)

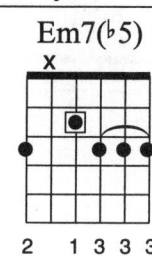
Em7(♭5)

Diminished 7 (1 ♭3 ♭5 ♭♭7)

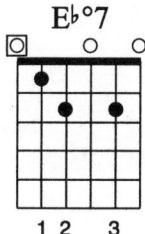
E♭°7

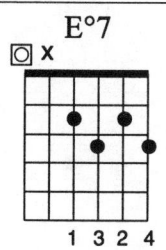
E°7

Augmented (1 3 #5)

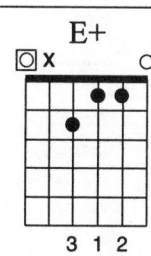
E+

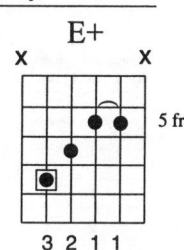
E+
5 fr

7(#5) (1 3 #5 ♭7)

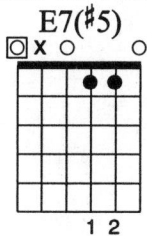
E7(#5)

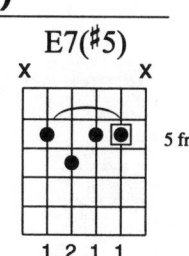
E7(#5)
5 fr

7(#9) (1 3 5 ♭7 #9)

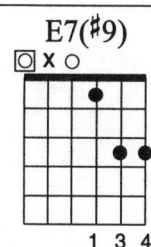
E7(#9)

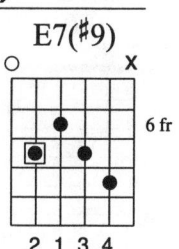
E7(#9)
6 fr

The F major scale:	F	G	A	Bb	C	D	E	F	G	A	Bb	C	D
	1	2	3	4	5	6	7	8	9	10	11	12	13

Major (1 3 5)

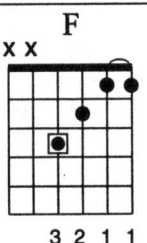 F

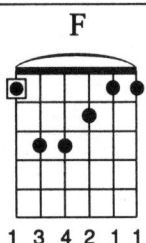 F

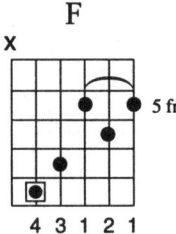 F

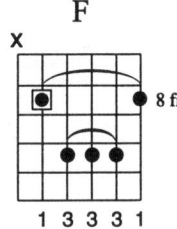 F

Minor (1 b3 5)

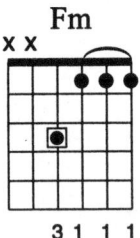 Fm

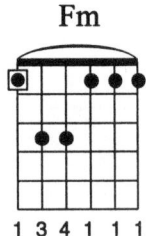 Fm

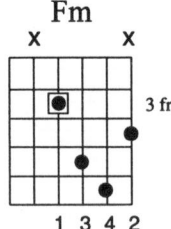 Fm

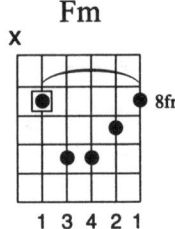 Fm

Dominant 7th (1 3 5 b7)

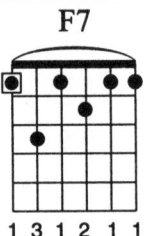 F7

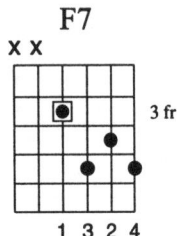 F7

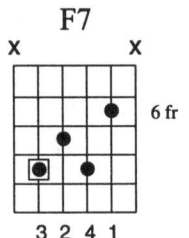 F7

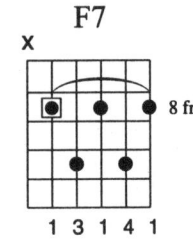 F7

Major 7 (1 3 5 7)

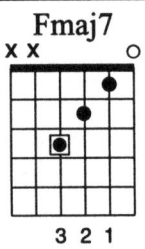 Fmaj7

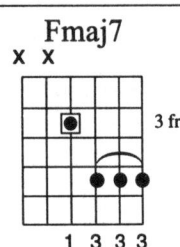 Fmaj7

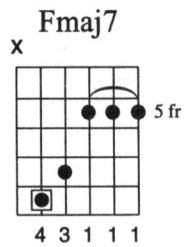 Fmaj7

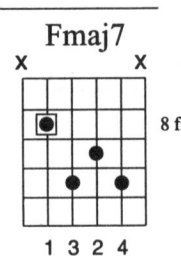 Fmaj7

Minor 7th (1 b3 5 b7)

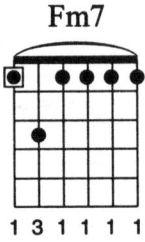 Fm7

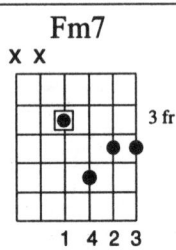 Fm7

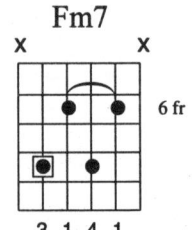 Fm7

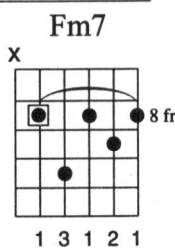 Fm7

Add 9 (1 3 5 9)

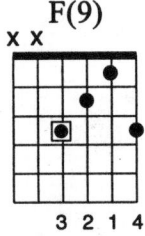 F(9)

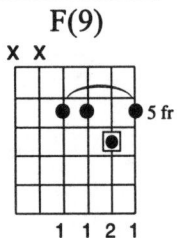 F(9)

Suspended 4 (1 4 5)

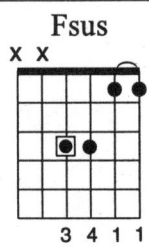 Fsus

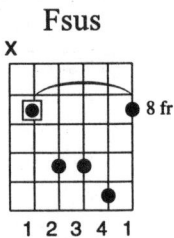 Fsus

The F major scale:	F	G	A	Bb	C	D	E	F	G	A	Bb	C	D
	1	2	3	4	5	6	7	8	9	10	11	12	13

Dominant 9 (1 3 5 b7 9)

F9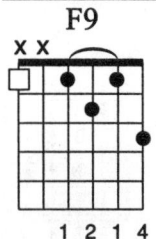

F9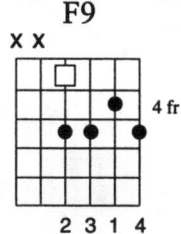

F9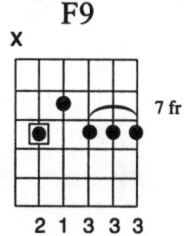

F9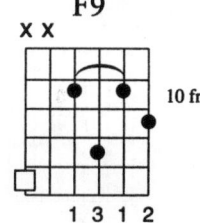

Dominant 13 (1 3 5 b7 13)

F13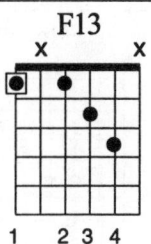

F13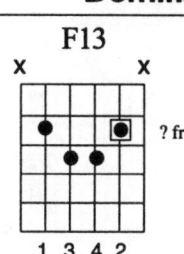

F13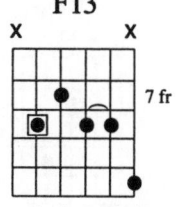

F13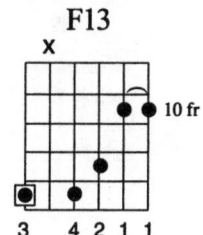

Dominant 7(b9) (1 3 5 b7 b9)

F7(b9)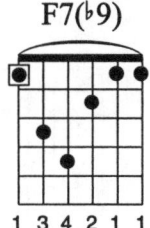

F7(b9)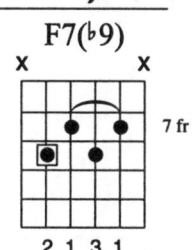

Major 6 (1 3 5 6)

F6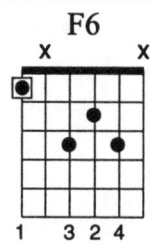

F6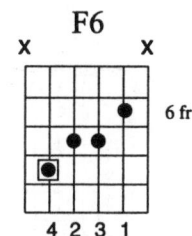

Minor 9 (1 b3 5 9)

Fm9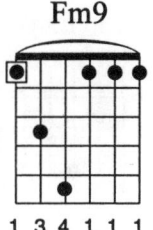

Fm9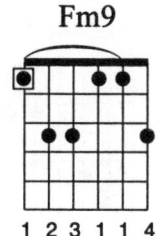

Minor 7(b5) (1 b3 b5 b7)

Fm7(b5)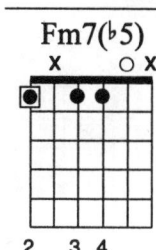

Fm7(b5)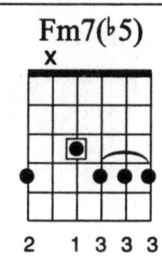

Diminished 7 (1 b3 b5 bb7)

F°7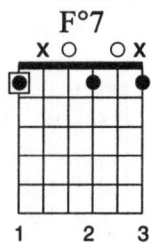

F°7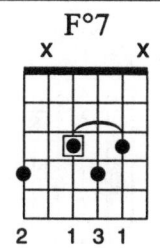

Augmented (1 3 #5)

F+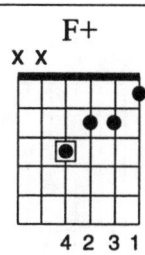

F+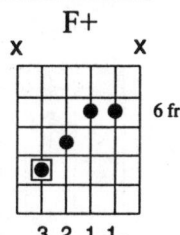

7(#5) (1 3 #5 b7)

F7(#5)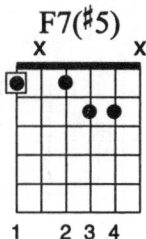

F7(#5)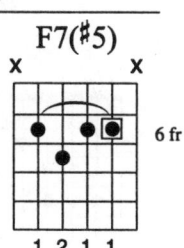

7(#9) (1 3 5 b7 #9)

F7(#9)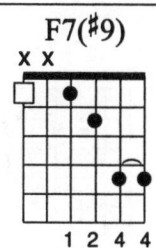

F7(#9)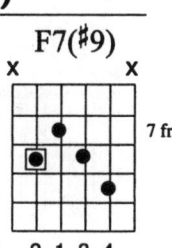

The F♯ major scale:	F♯	G♯	A♯	B	C♯	D♯	E♯	F♯	G♯	A♯	B	C♯	D♯
	1	2	3	4	5	6	7	8	9	10	11	12	13

Major (1 3 5)

F♯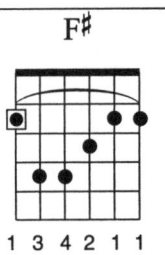
1 3 4 2 1 1

F♯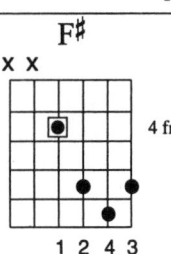
4 fr
1 2 4 3

F♯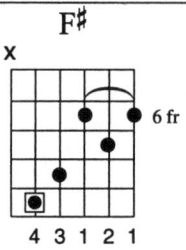
6 fr
4 3 1 2 1

F♯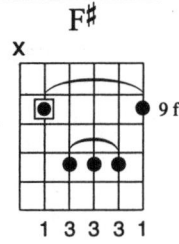
9 fr
1 3 3 3 1

Minor (1 ♭3 5)

F♯m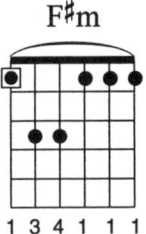
1 3 4 1 1 1

F♯m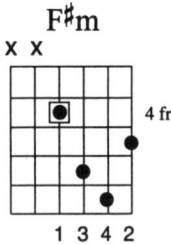
4 fr
1 3 4 2

F♯m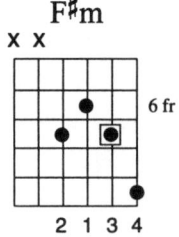
6 fr
2 1 3 4

F♯m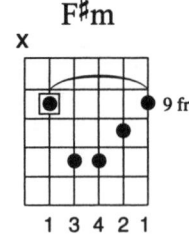
9 fr
1 3 4 2 1

Dominant 7th (1 3 5 ♭7)

F♯7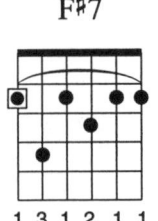
1 3 1 2 1 1

F♯7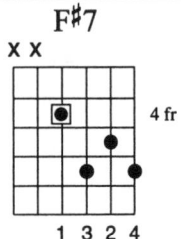
4 fr
1 3 2 4

F♯7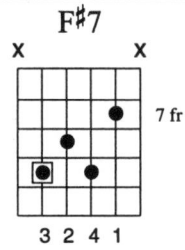
7 fr
3 2 4 1

F♯7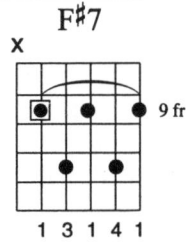
9 fr
1 3 1 4 1

Major 7 (1 3 5 7)

F♯maj7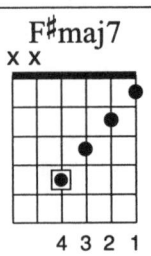
4 3 2 1

F♯maj7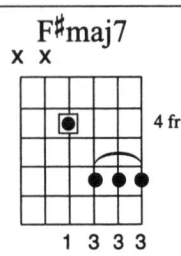
4 fr
1 3 3 3

F♯maj7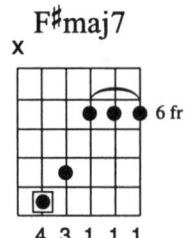
6 fr
4 3 1 1 1

F♯maj7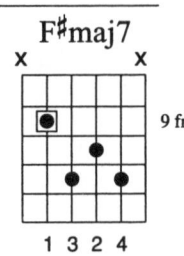
9 fr
1 3 2 4

Minor 7th (1 ♭3 5 ♭7)

F♯m7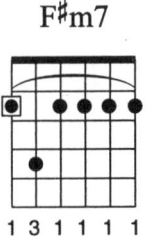
1 3 1 1 1 1

F♯m7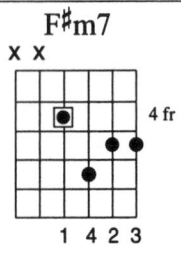
4 fr
1 4 2 3

F♯m7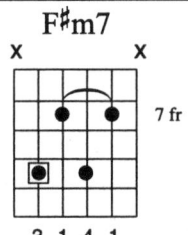
7 fr
3 1 4 1

F♯m7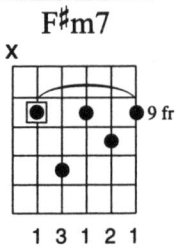
9 fr
1 3 1 2 1

Add 9 (1 3 5 9)

F♯(9)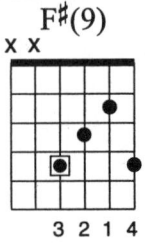
3 2 1 4

F♯(9)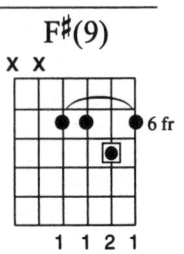
6 fr
1 1 2 1

Suspended 4 (1 4 5)

F♯sus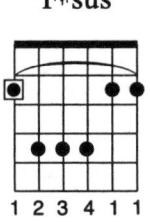
1 2 3 4 1 1

F♯sus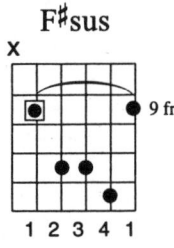
9 fr
1 2 3 4 1

The F♯ major scale:	F♯	G♯	A♯	B	C♯	D♯	E♯	F♯	G♯	A♯	B	C♯	D♯
	1	2	3	4	5	6	7	8	9	10	11	12	13

Dominant 9 (1 3 5 ♭7 9)

F♯9   F♯9   F♯9   F♯9

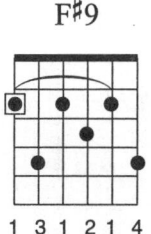 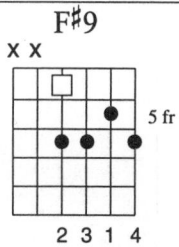 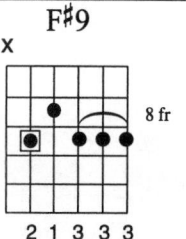 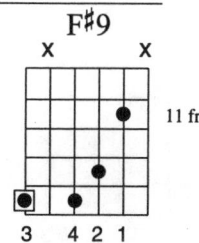

Dominant 13 (1 3 5 ♭7 13)

F♯13   F♯13   F♯13   F♯13

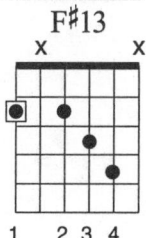 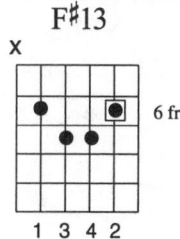 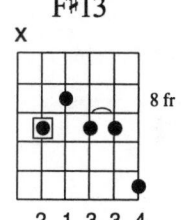 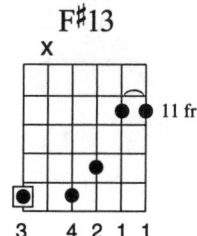

Dominant 7(♭9) (1 3 5 ♭7 ♭9)   Major 6 (1 3 5 6)

F♯7(♭9)   F♯7(♭9)   F♯6   F♯6

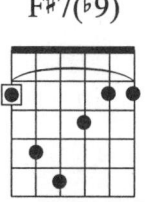 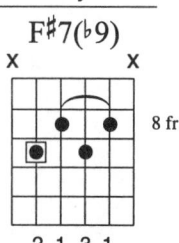 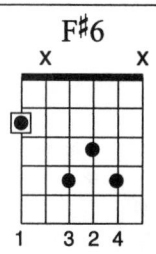 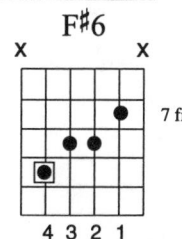

Minor 9 (1 ♭3 5 9)   Minor 7(♭5) (1 ♭3 ♭5 ♭7)

F♯m9   F♯m9   F♯m7(♭5)   F♯m7(♭5)

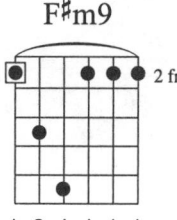 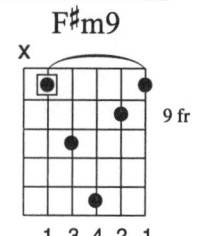 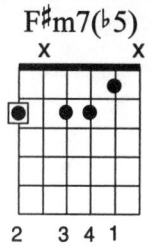 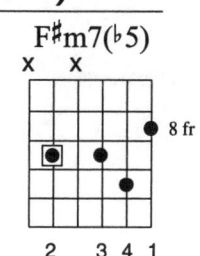

Diminished 7 (1 ♭3 ♭5 ♭♭7)   Augmented (1 3 ♯5)

F♯°7   F♯°7   F♯+   F♯+

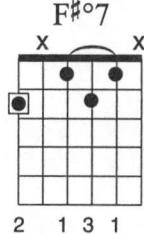 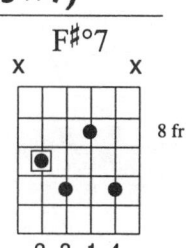 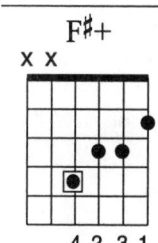 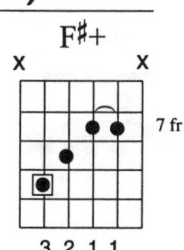

7(♯5) (1 3 ♯5 ♭7)   7(♯9) (1 3 5 ♭7 ♯9)

F♯7(♯5)   F♯7(♯5)   F♯7(♯9)   F♯7(♯9)

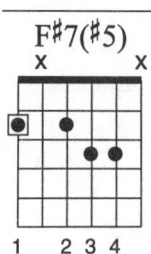 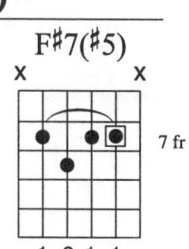 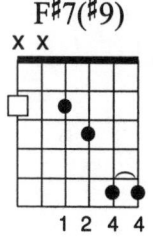 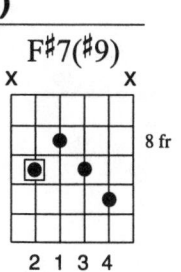

The G major scale:	G	A	B	C	D	E	F#	G	A	B	C	D	E
	1	2	3	4	5	6	7	8	9	10	11	12	13

Major (1 3 5)

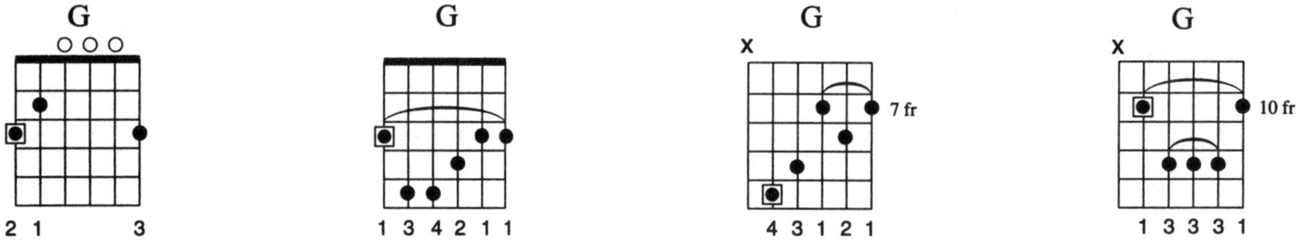

G G G G

Minor (1 ♭3 5)

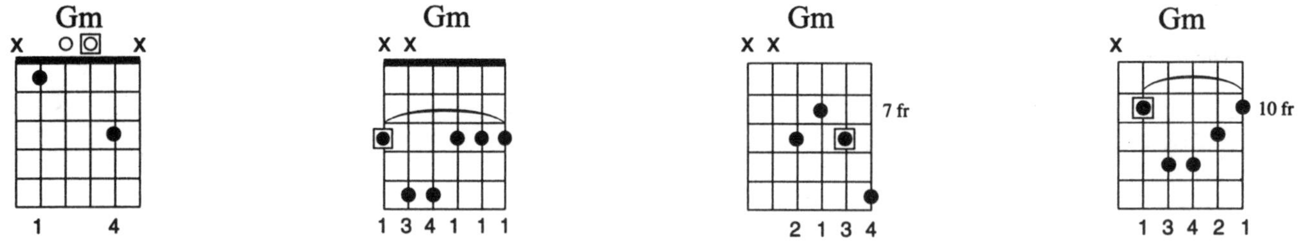

Gm Gm Gm Gm

Dominant 7th (1 3 5 ♭7)

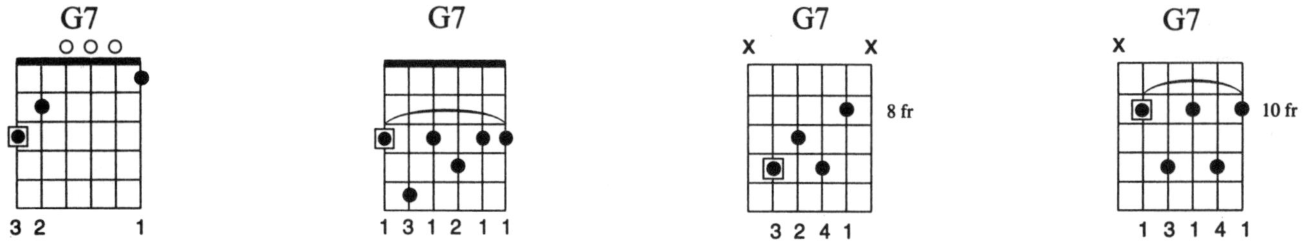

G7 G7 G7 G7

Major 7 (1 3 5 7)

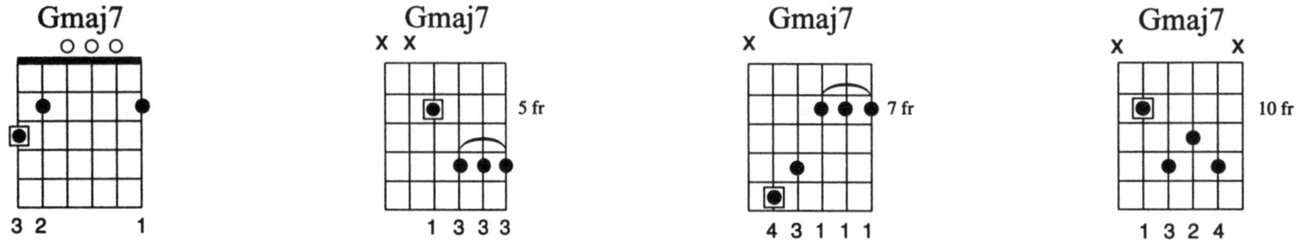

Gmaj7 Gmaj7 Gmaj7 Gmaj7

Minor 7th (1 ♭3 5 ♭7)

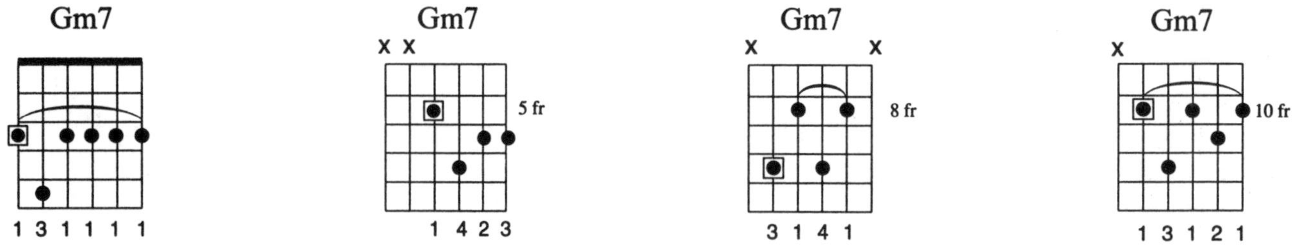

Gm7 Gm7 Gm7 Gm7

Add 9 (1 3 5 9)

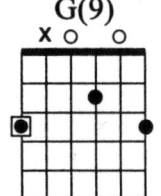
G(9)

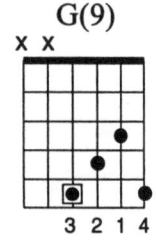
G(9)

Suspended 4 (1 4 5)

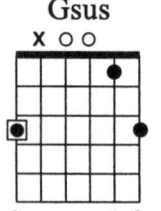
Gsus

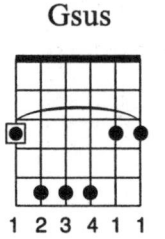
Gsus

The G major scale:	G	A	B	C	D	E	F#	G	A	B	C	D	E
	1	2	3	4	5	6	7	8	9	10	11	12	13

Dominant 9 (1 3 5 ♭7 9)

G9	G9	G9	G9
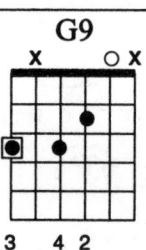	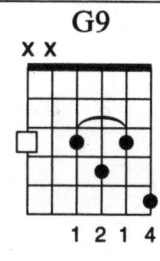	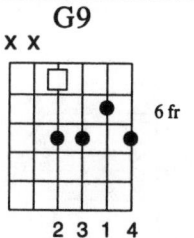	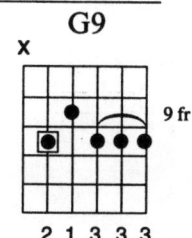

Dominant 13 (1 3 5 ♭7 13)

G13	G13	G13	G13
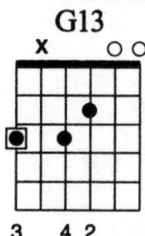	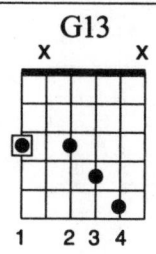	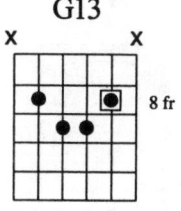	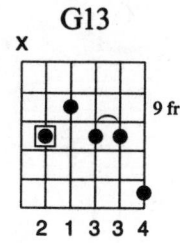

Dominant 7(♭9) (1 3 5 ♭7 ♭9)   ## Major 6 (1 3 5 6)

G7(♭9)	G7(♭9)	G6	G6
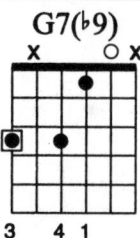	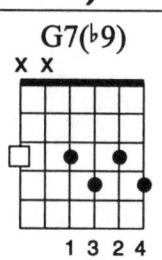	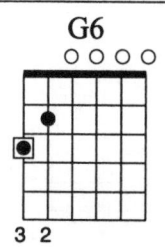	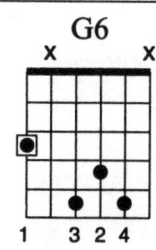

Minor 9 (1 ♭3 5 9)   ## Minor 7(♭5) (1 ♭3 ♭5 ♭7)

Gm9	Gm9	Gm7(♭5)	Gm7(♭5)
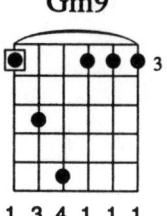	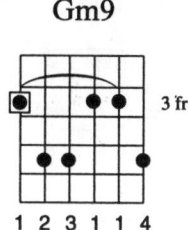	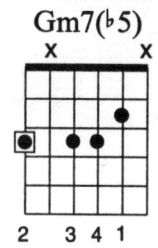	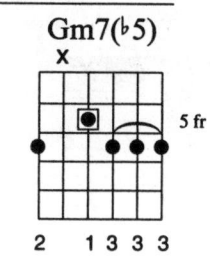

Diminished 7 (1 ♭3 ♭5 ♭♭7)   ## Augmented (1 3 ♯5)

G°7	G°7	G+	G+
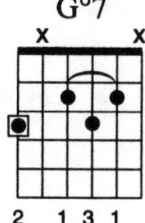	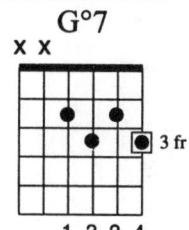	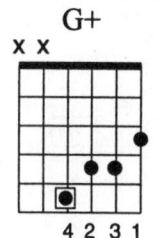	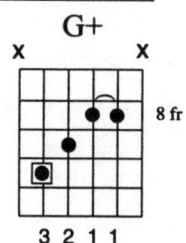

7(♯5) (1 3 ♯5 ♭7)   ## 7(♯9) (1 3 5 ♭7 ♯9)

G7(♯5)	G7(♯5)	G7(♯9)	G7(♯9)
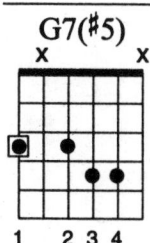	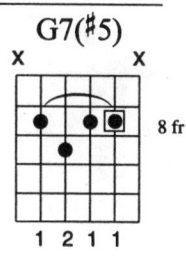	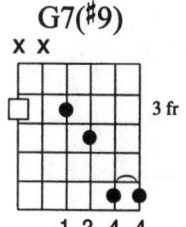	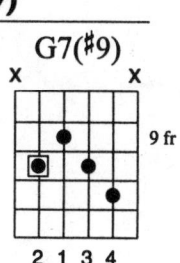

The A♭ major scale:	A♭	B♭	C	D	E♭	F	G	A♭	B♭	C	D	E♭	F
	1	2	3	4	5	6	7	8	9	10	11	12	13

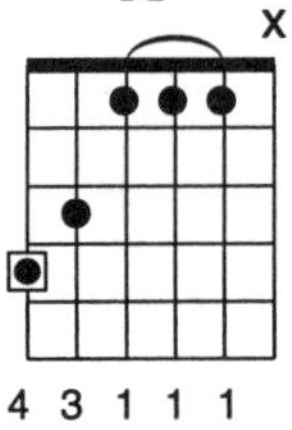

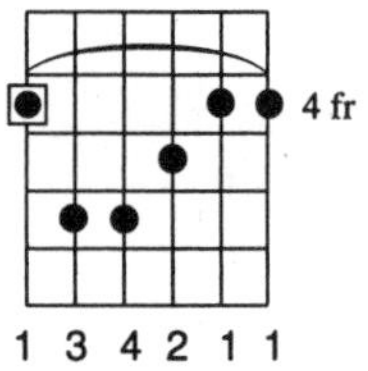

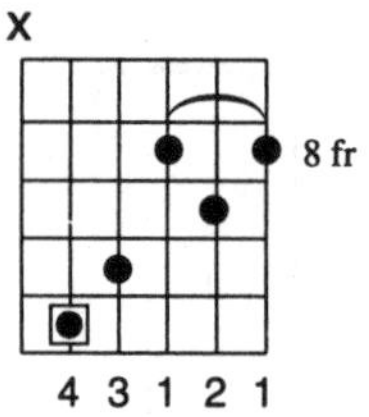

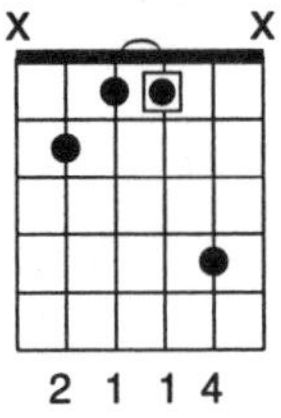

Major (1 3 5)

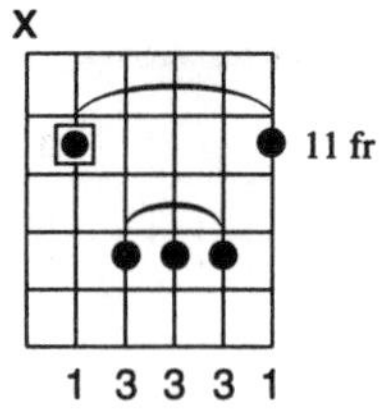

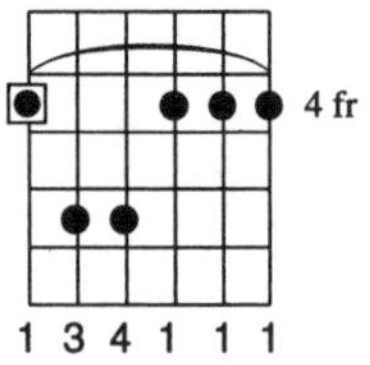

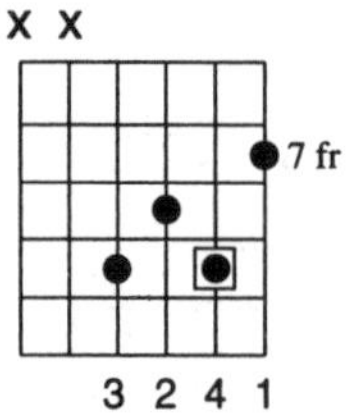

A♭

A♭

A♭

A♭

Minor (1 ♭3 5)

A♭m

A♭m

A♭m

A♭m

Dominant 7th (1 3 5 ♭7)

A♭7

A♭7

A♭7

A♭7

Major 7 (1 3 5 7)

A♭maj7

A♭maj7

A♭maj7

A♭maj7

Minor 7th (1 ♭3 5 ♭7)

A♭m7

A♭m7

A♭m7

A♭m7

Add 9 (1 3 5 9)

A♭(9)

A♭(9)

Suspended 4 (1 4 5)

A♭sus

A♭sus

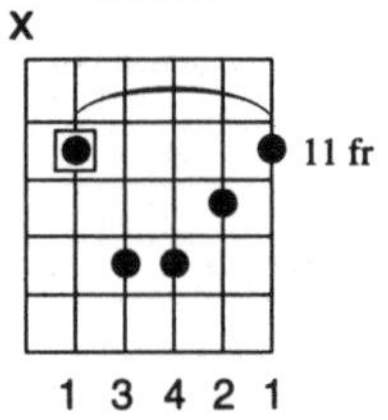

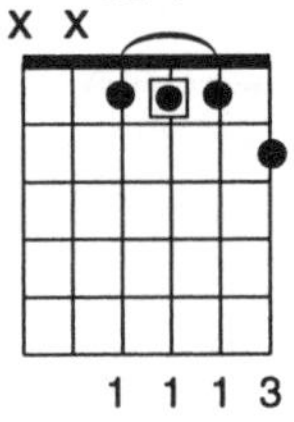

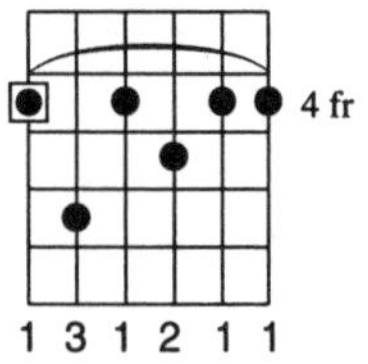

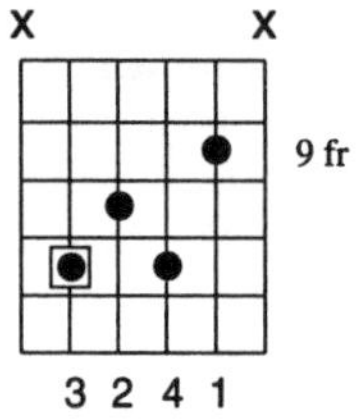

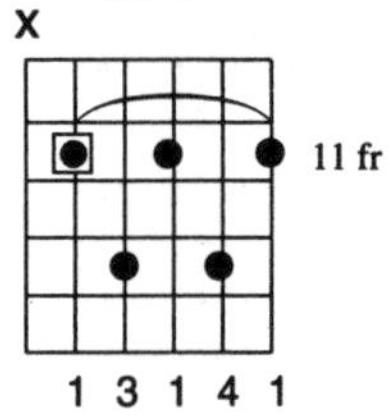

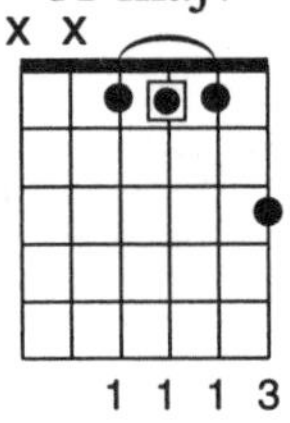

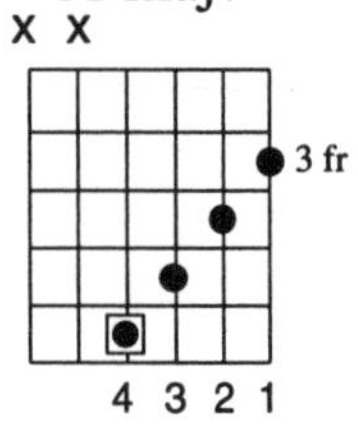

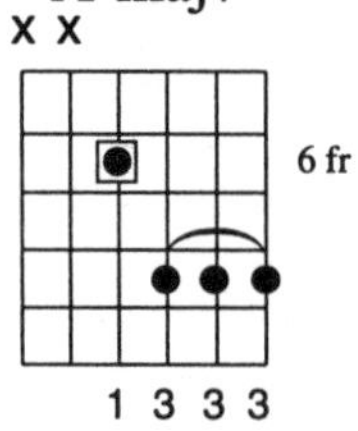

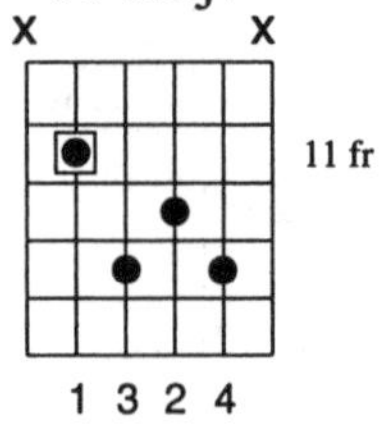

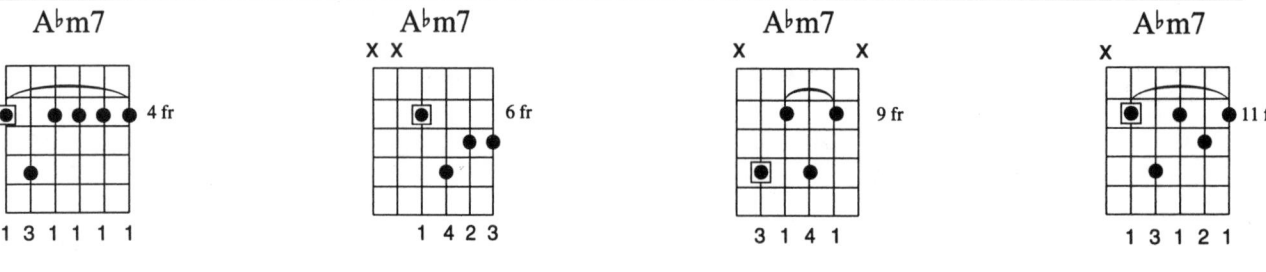

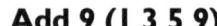

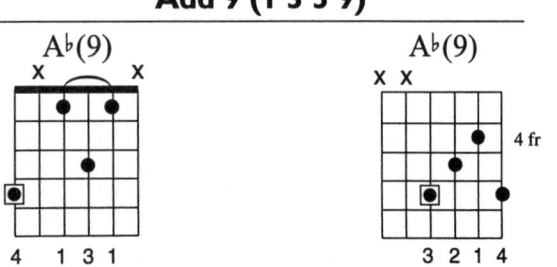

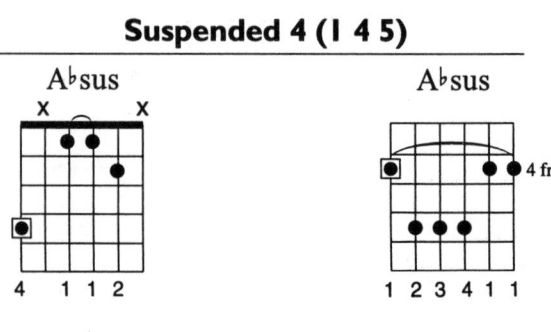